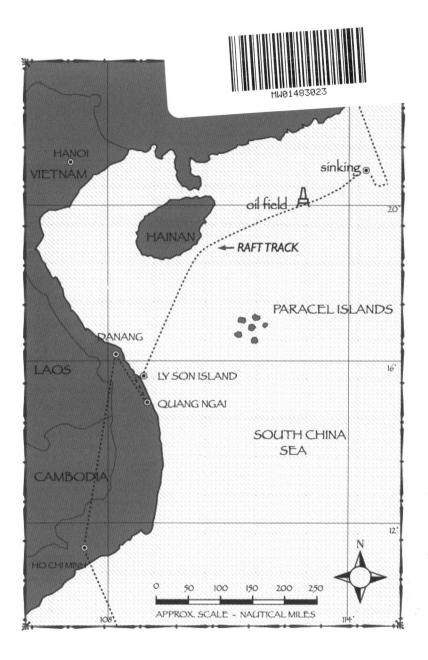

HANOI

VIETNAM

sinking ⊙

oil field

HAINAN

← RAFT TRACK

PARACEL ISLANDS

DANANG

LAOS

LY SON ISLAND

QUANG NGAI

SOUTH CHINA
SEA

CAMBODIA

HO CHI MINH

N

0   50   100   150   200   250

APPROX. SCALE - NAUTICAL MILES

i

Nautical Productions Pty Ltd

First published in Australia in 2007
by Nautical Productions Pty Ltd
ABN: 16 126 360 347

Nautical Productions Pty Ltd
PO Box 715, Moonah 7009, Tasmania, Australia.
Email: contact@tasplanet.com

Cataloguing-in-Publication data for this book is available from the
National Library of Australia:

ISBN 970-0-646-48041-1

Cover artwork: Bill Mearns

Printed and bound in Tasmania by Printing Authority of Australia
33 Innovation Drive
Dowsing Point
Tasmania 7010

BEYOND ALL LIMITS

A TRUE STORY

AN EPIC STORY OF THE AMAZING
SURVIVAL OF TWO MEN IN A LIFE RAFT

MARK SMITH

NAUTICAL PRODUCTIONS – *PUBLISHERS*

To Sophie and Daniel

My father has always taught me to have a healthy respect for the sea. Even though I grew up jumping on and off boats and running around the docks, I have always had an underlying fear of the deep blue unknown. I can never fathom how the sea can be so unrelenting, not caring whom she takes whether it is an experienced seaman or a child playing by the shore. I don't know if it was a fear of drowning or a fear of all the big bad things lurking under the surface but it was always there inside me.

Since my father's disappearance in December of 2005, I now know what my fear of the ocean is. It isn't drowning or being eaten by a shark, it is the unknown of the ocean, the ease at which people are stolen away from their loved ones, never to be seen again. That such a beautiful thing that provides so much enjoyment and a living for thousands across the world can turn on those who love it in the blink of an eye. The stories of survival on the ocean are pale in comparison to the tales of death and loss. But fortunately for my family and me, this book is a tale of survival. The survival of my father on the ocean he loves and has worked on for over 30 years… The ocean that tried its hardest to kill him for eleven long days.

Sophie Smith

Contents

Chapter

BEYOND ALL LIMITS
A TRUE STORY

Introduction

It all started innocently enough. I had just finished a couple of months of tuna fishing on the F.V. *Ocean Dawn*. I had given up full-time long-lining a few years ago, but was always happy to fill in when my good friend and owner of DeBretts Seafood, Stephen Davis, needed a relief captain and fishing master. I was standing on his wharf in Mooloolaba on the Sunshine Coast in southern Queensland, wondering what to do next. Christmas was just a few weeks away.

My mobile phone rang. It was Kurt. "Mark, can you deliver my motor yacht, like, from Hong Kong to Sydney before Christmas?" I said yes, for two reasons. Firstly, the project was not unfamiliar to me. It had been planned and budgeted several months ago but had been put on hold for various reasons, and secondly because of my sea experience. I had been in command of all types of small craft since 1984. For the past twenty-one years I had battled monster seas off Tasmania's west and south coasts and had survived the eyes of two category five cyclones in the South Pacific. I had fished and delivered vessels around the entire coastline of Australia, and sailed countless thousands of nautical miles in pursuit of the elusive tuna. My adventures covered the great Southern Ocean, the North and South Indian Ocean, the South Atlantic Ocean, the South Pacific Ocean the Tasman Sea, the Solomon Sea, the Coral Sea and the Andaman Sea. I was in no doubt of my abilities and I thought I had seen and survived everything the ocean could throw at me. How wrong could I have been?

Departing Australia

That fateful call was at 1200 hours on the 25th of November 2005. The vessel owner, Kurt Braun, was at that moment organising to fly us to Hong Kong the next day, departing from Sydney's Kingsford Smith Airport. That gave me twenty-four hours to clean up the master's cabin and bridge of the *Ocean Dawn*, pack, drive to Brisbane and fly to Sydney; and of course, I had to find a crewmember willing to come at such short notice. This last task was easy. Stephen Freeman, who had sailed with me on many occasions and had been a member of my crew for the last few months, immediately agreed. Stephen was a physically tough and hardened seaman – no 'yachtie' here.

Stephen had his own reasons for joining me. The tuna industry was in serious trouble, with all stakeholders (owners, factories and crews) unsure of their futures. The $5,000 I offered him was substantially more than he could earn from a month's fishing. It would give him the opportunity to finance his return to his home in New Zealand.

After a busy afternoon and evening finishing my chores and calling my young brother Andrew and my children Sophie and Daniel to tell them what I was doing, I slept early. Steve's friend Gail had kindly offered to drive us to Brisbane Airport. We had agreed to meet at 0730 so that we would have plenty of time for the hour's drive to the airport to catch our 1015 flight to Sydney. Nevertheless, due to Steve and Gail having a late night out on the town, we were running late when we arrived at the airport and had to make a run for the plane. Within minutes of finding our seats, we were climbing out over Moreton Bay on our way to Sydney and the international airport.

At the international ticket counter we came up against our first problem – no tickets. A quick call to Kurt and he was on his way to sort things out. Tiny alarm bells started to ring in my head. Firstly, the tickets that Kurt had said were paid for clearly were not. Secondly, once Kurt had arrived and we waited for his credit card transaction, Kurt gave me $5,000 as a float to start preparation work on his vessel. The ticketing staff then told him that his credit card had not been accepted, the result being that Kurt then asked for most of the cash back, to pay for our tickets. It struck me as odd, that this supposedly rich man did not have sufficient funds to start an expensive delivery voyage. Our budget, completed months before, had indicated an approximate budget of $80,000 Australian.

After the tickets were finally issued we had about thirty minutes before we had to proceed to the departure lounge; enough time for a coffee and a 'get to know you' chat with Kurt. I hurriedly signed the contract he placed in front of me, agreeing to deliver his vessel for the sum of $17,000 Australian. Kurt gave us directions to his vessel in Hong Kong. From the airport we were to catch a taxi to the Aberdeen Yacht Club, then catch a sampan and find the boat on a mooring in the bay. The local boat boy would be waiting for us. It sounded simple enough.

All of this took longer than the thirty minutes we had to spare, and before we knew it we heard calls over the PA system for a Mr Mark Smith and Mr Stephen Freeman to proceed immediately to the boarding gate. We made a mad rush for the gate, where we were picked up by a slightly annoyed but pleasant Qantas staff member, who rushed us through immigration and customs and bundled us on to the aircraft with seconds to spare. From some of the looks we received on board, it was obvious that we had held up the whole show. Never mind, we were now safe and sound in our seats. Within the next few minutes we were airborne and grinning. I said to Steve, "Well mate, in a few hours we're going to be in Hong Kong!"

Hong Kong

Being an outdoors type and someone who hates flying, it was with great relief that I heard the pilot say, "We are starting our descent, belt up everyone. Hong Kong here we come," or words to that effect. We went through the normal routine at the airport and after a bit of circle work we found the taxi rank. We climbed into the first one and I informed the driver, "Aberdeen Yacht Club" which was met by a blank look and no response. So I tried again in Chinese, "Aberdeenie Yachtie Clubie, please." I received the same response but nevertheless, we were on the move. After the driver made many phone calls and stops we eventually found our way and were dropped outside the above-mentioned club. It was midnight.

We walked up and down the road looking for a pathway to the waterfront. We eventually made our way through a maze of small workshops filled with all sorts of marine parts and machinery – gearboxes, diesel engines, pumps, lathes, welding machines and more. There were groups of men sitting around low tables playing cards and mahjong, and smoking and eating. They all glanced up at us, surprised to see two Western men struggling with their luggage as they negotiated the littered alleyways. We made it to the water, only to be confronted with at least a thousand vessels on moorings. I asked Steve, "Bloody oath, how are we going to find our boat in that lot?"

There were two young boys fishing from a small jetty. With lots of pointing and gesticulating, they understood that we wanted to get out to our vessel. In response to a few shouts and whistles, a sampan miraculously appeared. We jumped on board and I pointed out towards the labyrinth of boats.

Kurt had told me approximately where his boat was, but it took us an hour of searching before we spotted the stern of a vessel that looked about right. After pushing through a tangle of mooring lines we jumped on board Kurt's vessel and were greeted by Eddy, the boat boy. Well, he wasn't exactly a boy. I put his age at about forty-five years or so. He seemed a nice chap and after giving us a quick cook's tour, concentrating on the generator and power systems, he left us to it and said he would be back in the morning.

On first impressions, it was a very 'flash Harry' type of boat; lots of leather, chrome and polished timber. Steve took the guest cabin in the bow and I took the master's cabin in the stern. It was very comfortable, with an island double bed, recessed lighting everywhere, and more polished timber and chrome. It also had an ensuite containing a bath, shower, toilet and bidet. It was a very comfy nest. It was about

0200 hours in the morning, so after a stroll around the decks, taking in the lights and the smells of Hong Kong at night, we retired to bed. I slept like a baby and was awake and showered when Eddy returned as promised at about 0900 hours the next morning.

We spent the next two hours going over the vessel in detail. After the inspection I thought that with a bit of work I could get to know the yacht well enough to make a safe passage. It was also clear to me that Eddy knew how to wash and polish his charge, but very little else. He did, however, ask a question that I found a bit odd. He asked, "What are you men doing here?"

I said, "That should be obvious Eddy, we are delivering this boat to Sydney for Kurt. I thought you knew that."

He replied, "You guys are mad."

"What do you mean by that? It's five reasonably short legs; the longest being eight hundred nautical miles, the shortest four hundred and fifty nautical miles, mostly in sight of land. What's the problem?" He just sort of smiled and we left it at that. Eddy said his goodbyes and promised to come back to help the next morning. I figured he was just scared of the deep blue unknown.

I went ashore and called Kurt from a pay phone. I told him we had arrived safely and that I was happy with my initial inspections. I also said I needed money to start our preparations and make purchases to get the boat seaworthy and ready to depart.

And so started a busy week, methodically checking that all of the yacht's systems and engine components were in good working order and making lists of items in need of repair or replacement. Eddy worked for the boat yard where Kurt had a long-established working relationship, so whatever we needed he was able to arrange. The first thing we did was make a list of spares and parts for the engine room, and Eddy arranged for batteries and parts to be delivered and fitted by the shipyard's engineers, as well as for delivery of the other spare parts.

I spent most of the first day in the engine room, checking the twin V16 Detroit two-stroke diesel motors and cleaning and oiling an offending junction box with Steve's help. There were clouds of white smoke coming from the starboard engine, most likely because the engines hadn't been run regularly and worked to their design loads. The worst thing you can do to engines and boats in general is just to let them sit idle without working; this can cause all sorts of problems. Starting a diesel motor once a week, as Eddy had probably been doing, and letting it idle for a few minutes before shutting it down can cause more harm than good. Nevertheless, the exhaust didn't worry me greatly; a good run during sea trials would deglaze the bores and seat the rings a bit better. By the end of the day I had the engines both running with a nice harmonic balance; two powerful engines running with a steady throb deep in the heart of the boat.

I turned to Steve who had been working alongside me all day. "Well mate, she sounds sweet. I reckon that's enough for the day. Let's shut down, clean up and go find a beer."

"Sounds good to me, big fella," said Steve.

Half an hour later, dressed up sharp, we hailed a sampan and settled down for the trip across the harbour to the suburb of Aberdeen. The traffic on the water was hectic, boats of all shapes and sizes creating a slop that the sampan ducked and plunged in. We passed one of the most famous floating restaurants in the world, and the Aberdeen Yacht Club filled with gleaming super yachts. We passed countless fishing vessels all moored midstream, with people fishing and living and going about their daily business.

We jumped ashore and wandered into the main shopping centre of Aberdeen (a suburb of Hong Kong). I do enjoy being thrown into a totally different environment and culture. From the most remote tribes in the Solomon Sea to the massive metropolises of Tokyo and Calcutta, or the danger zones of Port Moresby and Cape Town; all of my journeys have been as a fisherman, never as a tourist, so there are no hotel bookings or half-day bus tours. I just hop off my boat and march straight in at street level.

Around and around we went, past countless small shops filled with all sorts of Oriental wares and merchandise. My first job was to buy a mobile phone. We found a little shop on a corner where the Chinese owner spoke English, and after a bit of haggling I was back in contact with the outside world. There was still no bar in sight or anything that looked even remotely like one. Steve found the name of a bar in the Wan Chai district, so off we went in a taxi, taking in the sights, through the Aberdeen Tunnel, past the Hong Kong Jockey Club and into central Hong Kong.

The traffic. Man, there is one thing I do know about my life, I could never live in a big city. The traffic, vehicular and pedestrian, would send me around the bend. Exciting to visit, but to live there? No! Still, there was plenty to look at and we had a good view of Hong Kong as we inched along. We climbed out of the taxi in front of the Laguna Club.

We ordered a beer at the bar and found ourselves a table with a view of proceedings. I nearly choked on my first swig. I was gob smacked. "Holy shit!" I said to Steve.

The place was full of the most beautiful girls God could ever have created. Before we knew it, we were surrounded with all avenues of retreat blocked off by six delightfully happy girls, Florida, Malan, Susie, Kristie, Anna and Mary. My first thoughts that maybe this was a house of ill repute were quickly put to rest. This was a popular bar where the women, mostly domestic workers, came to see if they could find a decent Western man. Looking around, there were a few Western men at the bar, mostly older business types, but all with that distinctly married look about them. The girls, after a lot of convincing, were more than happy to find out that we were completely and utterly single. Fishing life does not usually allow for anything else. We made instant friends and settled down to a great night of eating, drinking, dancing and chatting about everything in general.

The girls were great company. They were all from the Philippines and were either employed or seeking employment as domestic workers in Hong Kong. They told us of their lives at home, of how they were helping to support their families because employment in the rice fields had become virtually non-existent. This was the only way they could find employment and send money to their families to supplement shortages at home. They spoke of their contracts, the agency fees and their difficulties obtaining visas. It sounded to me as if the agency had the upper hand, and was no better than a loan shark, exploiting these beautiful people. But I kept my thoughts to myself.

Malan had taken an instant liking to Steve and vice versa, and they were getting along very well. I had noticed that Florida was the mother hen of the group and could sense the level of care and compassion she displayed towards her friends. I was enjoying her company. At first I thought she was the same age as all her friends, somewhere in her mid-twenties, until she proudly announced that she was thirty-nine years old. This was a pleasant shock really, as I was forty-nine at the time.

After another long day working through the checklists on the boat, we caught up with the girls again the following evening and being free the following day, Florida and Malan came back with us to the yacht. They were more than impressed with Kurt's boat and ran around all excited, checking things out. I have to say that it was as good as a five-star hotel. Steve made us all a coffee and we sat in the saloon, listening to music and chatting. Before I knew it, Steve and Malan had disappeared, leaving Florida and myself alone. A few minutes later we had cuddled up in bed, shared a goodnight kiss and slept peacefully in each other's arms.

The next few days were a blur of hard work and pleasant times socialising with Florida and Malan. When they weren't working at their jobs they would come by to see us. They set about cleaning the saloon and cabins and had the entire interior of the boat shining like a new pin, dusted, polished and tidied, right down to creaseless beds and shining mirrors. I barely recognised my cabin and wondering what had happened to all my gear, found my socks and underwear in the drawers of the dresser. Even my jocks were folded! My shirts, jeans and trousers were all on coat hangers and my shoes were in a row on the floor on one side, my empty sea bag folded on the other. I have spent the last fifteen years basically living on fishing vessels, fending for myself, so this was a new experience, and definitely cool. The bathroom was no exception, with scrubbed tiles and folded towels and all of my gear neatly laid out.

I spent most of our second day in Hong Kong on the bridge, going over all the navigation equipment or, as I discovered, the lack of it. There was no GPS (satellite-derived global positioning system), no radar, no computerised plotting system, no depth sounder, no radios, no charts, clock, barometer or parallel rules; not even a pencil. The only items of bridge equipment were an old autopilot and a steering compass. I also discovered that the rudder feedback unit was totally rusted and broken, and without this piece of equipment, the autopilot would be totally useless. The chances of finding a spare for this relic were next to nothing so unless a miracle happened, it looked like hand steering. This was not a disaster, it would just make the voyage so much harder. But while I could live without an autopilot, without radar, and in fact, without most of the items that I usually associated with a well-equipped bridge, I could not live without radios or a GPS. Fitting out the high-frequency radio and the GPS plotter would be a simple affair. Basically, I had to find a suitable power source mount and connect the cables and turn them on. Eddy turned up at that point as if on cue, and after I explained what I needed he said that he would come back in the morning and take us to his friend who owned a marine electronics shop.

Reporting in to Kurt, he was enthusiastic and happy with the day's progress. He readily agreed to my arguments about the electronics purchases and asked me to call his secretary, Elizabeth, to make the necessary funds transfers, which I did. I also took the opportunity to inform Elizabeth of my budgetary needs, to enable departure from Hong Kong on time. With all my purchases and the 10,000 litres of fuel required, I was going to need approximately $17,000 Australian within the next few days. She said she would make the arrangements.

That evening, Florida and Malan laid on a feast. I couldn't remember eating so well and to complement the food, Steve had discovered Kurt's stash of wine, a bottle of which he donated to the proceedings. We enjoyed good company, fine food and fine wine, and finished up with ice cream on the aft deck, washed down with tequila, orange juice and crushed ice. It was a great night. Both Florida and Malan were busy the next day so sadly, we had to end the evening. Before leaving on the sampan, I gave Florida a hug and a kiss to sleep well, and promised to call her the following day. She said she would like that, and I went to sleep totally happy.

The next morning, Eddy and I set off in a sampan to an island on the other side of Aberdeen Harbour. This was a miniature city in itself – apartment blocks, office towers, shops and a busy, crowded community at street level. Eddy told me that this was a place in Hong Kong that supports the marine industry and this became apparent as we made our way through the maze of streets. There was everything a seaman could want – anchors, chains, rope, pumps, safety gear, lubricants, paints, fastenings, hoses and much, much more. Eddy took me to one of the many shops selling electronic equipment and introduced me to the owner, a very polite and happy Chinese gentleman, Mr Kim, who spoke fluent English. I briefed him on the upcoming delivery voyage, and asked if he could quote and supply and fit my electronic requirements: a high frequency single sideband marine radio with all allowable frequencies and coupled to this an automatic aerial tuner and a twenty foot whip antenna, plus a waterproof, hand-held VHF; and a GPS plotting unit. Whether by good luck or good fortune, the shop stocked the Coden brand of radios that I was familiar with, and a compact GPS plotter unit with a six inch screen, which had all the features I required. Mr Kim was happy to supply and fit the order as soon as payment was made, and promised to have his technicians start installation the following morning.

While I was doing all of this, Steve had been checking the safety and survival gear and when I arrived back on the boat, he had all the safety gear he could find laid out ready for inspection. It looked like we would have to make another shopping list! We had an RFD brand self-inflating life raft certified for six people. It was due for its next periodic survey in one month's time; close, but acceptable. It was housed in a canvas bag and we stowed it in one of the aft lockers where it would be readily accessible. Next there was a box of flares, most of which were out of date and would need replacing. There were a dozen or so serviceable old life belts but without whistles and lights, and that was about it. It was another long shopping list – new flares, (rockets, red hand-held and orange smokes) lights and whistles for the life belts, two life rings with heaving lines, a 'man overboard' strobe light, first aid kit, fire extinguishers, fire blankets, torches with plenty of batteries, globes, matches, glue and sundry items needed or useful in an emergency. On the bottom of the list I wrote EPIRB – emergency position indicating radio beacon. Simply put, when activated, these units send out a radio signal on a preset wavelength. This alerts global search and rescue operations of its position, making rescue pretty much assured. I had never sailed without one since they entered general service about twenty years ago.

The next morning the electronics technicians arrived to install the radio and GPS unit. When they finished, the black numbers of the LED display were clearly visible – 2182, the international distress frequency. Turning to the GPS plotter, the red ship's icon was placed metre perfect over our position in a blown up chart of Aberdeen Harbour.

Eddy and his mate, the chief engineer, were impressed with my new toys on the bridge and spent a few minutes poking their noses around the new acquisitions. Then I sat down with the chief and discussed my most pressing need – fuel. The sea trials would hopefully confirm my maths but I had calculated a fuel burn of 50 litres an hour per engine, running slightly over idle. To cover the longest leg with adequate reserves, I had estimated that we would have to carry a minimum amount of 10,000 litres. The boat held 7,000 litres in two tanks, so I would need on-deck storage for a further 3,000 litres. The chief said he could supply three 1,000 litre plastic containers reinforced by an outer steel mesh.

As evening fell, Florida (who had come to visit earlier) and I caught a sampan across the harbour to find somewhere to eat. We were happily chatting when we entered the restaurant and we were still happily talking when we left. It was like we had known each other forever. We just wandered along with the mass of people that made up Hong Kong, going in no particular direction or with any destination in mind. We went past a club with a live band and ended up slow dancing in each other's arms. At about eleven o'clock we said good night and I promised to call her the next day to organise the plans for the sea trials. I jumped a taxi and was lucky to catch the last sampan on the Aberdeen waterfront. On the way across the harbour, I couldn't help thinking that Florida's goodnight kiss lasted a little bit longer than the ones before. I was definitely enjoying one of the happiest times of my life.

When I called Florida the following day, she was all excited about the trials and was looking forward to seeing me again. Just before we hung up she told me she missed me. Crikey! No one had missed me since I got lost at the zoo when I was five years old!

One important job I had to do was to arrange suitable insurance for the voyage. This was for two reasons – firstly, to protect Kurt's investment and secondly, the Hong Kong authorities would not grant port clearance without valid insurance papers. To obtain insurance the boat had to be surveyed and valued. Kurt had given me the number of the boat broker who had sold him the boat, a man called Peter who was also an insurance agent and should be able to help. I called the number and after introducing myself, explained my business in Hong Kong. Peter was cheerful with a polished British accent. He listened to my enquiry and immediately offered to help. He had done business with Kurt previously and had all the files and old survey and valuation reports in his office. He suggested using the same surveyor who had done the work when Kurt was negotiating to buy the boat, which seemed the logical thing to do. Peter understood the urgency and agreed to meet me on the boat with a surveyor who he named, first thing in the morning.

When I briefed Kurt on the progress with the insurance he was happy until I mentioned who the surveyor was and his attitude changed abruptly. Under no circumstances was I to use this surveyor and I was to call Peter immediately to arrange a replacement. I argued that this surveyor was familiar with the boat, which would save a lot of time and money, to the extent that he may simply need to update his files on the vessel, but Kurt wouldn't budge. Wondering what that was all about, I called Peter. He was a bit surprised but respected Kurt's decision. He told me he would see what he could do at such short notice.

When Peter called back, he told me he had organised a different surveyor – a British mariner, an ex-Royal Navy chap. When I reported this back to Kurt he was as happy as, back to his old self. He was more than pleased that preparations were progressing well and that I was still on schedule to depart in a few days' time. He was looking forward to cruising on Sydney Harbour with his friends over Christmas. Tomorrow would be the survey and fueling, the sea trials the next and then we would be nearly there. If all kept going well, we would have a third, final day of last minute purchasing and clearances and we would be on our way to the Philippines.

On the morning of the surveyor's inspection we decided that Steve might as well take the day off. He arranged to meet up with Malan and went off happily with a part payment of his agreed fee and a few hundred dollars for food and refreshments for the upcoming sea trials.

In my eyes the boat was looking shipshape – it was spotless, and everything was in its place. The finishing touch was to use the freshwater hose to wash away the night's grime from the topsides and wet the teak decks down. The driftwood grey decks sprung to life in a golden glow; they looked beautiful. I settled down to wait for Peter and his mate to arrive.

Peter was just as I had expected; on time, immaculately dressed in expensive nautical garb, friendly and terribly correct – all the basic necessities for a super yacht salesman. He introduced me to Brian, the surveyor. On first impressions he had the look of an experienced seaman; a large, rather rotund and cheery man. He had a ruddy face and a seaman's beard. It was impossible to miss the faded sailor's tattoos on his arms. We were all young once.

Peter was a successful, professional international super yacht broker and Brian an ex-Royal Navy veteran who specialised in engineering. There was respect all around. I was keen to learn more about the super yacht industry as I'd had a long-term dream to move in this direction. Peter was full of information and encouragement, even mentioning a shortage of skilled captains and officers. This was music to my ears. Could this be the first step towards my dream?

After preliminaries we started on the formal stuff. In order to obtain insurance, I had to provide two things. Firstly, the vessel had to be in a suitably seaworthy state to undertake the planned voyage and secondly, the qualifications and experience of the master, myself, had to be deemed sufficient to the undertaking. It was up to the marine surveyor to be the judge of these matters. We started with me and I handed Brian copies of my current and up-to-date tickets. The USL code Skipper grade 2 and USL code Master four, Marine

Engine Driver grade three, my radio operator's licence and a current senior first aid certificate. I supported these documents with my most precious possession, my sea service record book dating back to 1984, and my current and expired passports that could track my history from 1985. To tie it all together, I handed the surveyor a copy of my CV, and took this opportunity to pass another copy to Peter, which he happily accepted. Armed with this information, Brian could accurately trace my history back twenty years or more and follow the path of my seagoing career. All my study and examinations have taken place at the Australian Maritime College located close to the mouth of the Tamar River in beautiful northern Tasmania – the premier and most picturesque marine learning centre in Australia.

In 1984 I had obtained my unrestricted coxswain's ticket, which meant I could skipper my then new 8.5 metre aluminium fishing boat around the entire coastline of Tasmania out to thirty miles. In 1990, I qualified as a Skipper grade 5, and could command fishing vessels up to twenty-five metres to offshore limits of two hundred nautical miles. In 1996 I became a Skipper grade 2, and was able to captain all fishing vessels up to 35 metres for unlimited operations and captain fishing vessels up to eighty metres to offshore limits of two hundred nautical miles. I could also be chief mate of fishing or trading vessels up to eighty metres to coastal and middle water limits (six hundred nautical miles) and watch keeper on fishing vessels up to three thousand gross tons or one hundred metres in length for unlimited operations. In 2005 I passed the Master four examinations. This allowed me to captain trading vessels up to eighty metres in in-shore limits and captain trading vessels of 35 metres in middle water limits operation. It was in the six and ten year gaps between attending college that all of the real learning took place – at sea. To move up through the ranks you have to serve a minimum amount of approved sea time, which takes years to accumulate. I was proud of my Master four certificate and for the past two years I had served as master on a number of ocean-going salvage tugs. I was engaged in all sorts of interesting and challenging projects – complicated multiple tows, marine construction, salvage work and scientific expeditions. This had been my first step out of fishing and into the world of commercial and trading vessels, hopefully leading my way to the white boat industry. A few months previously I had logged on to a few crew agency companies in America, searching for positions.

Brian was more than happy with the information I gave him. We chatted over several items as he leafed through it all. He stopped at one of the entries. "Ah! Port Blair. I have been there, we were on a goodwill cruise and guests of the Indian Navy."

We had something in common, which was good. I spoke to him of my experience there. Port Blair is the capital city of the Andaman Islands. They are a low-lying string of jewels floating in the Torquays and tranquil Andaman Sea. Owned by India but contested by a not-friendly Burma, there was a strong Indian military presence, notably, a large naval base, in the harbour. It was basically a 'no go' area for all except the most stubborn backpacker. Not being a bona fide tourist when I was there, I was quickly put under house arrest until special permission was granted for me to board the fishing vessel, *Sumanatra*, as captain and fishing master, three days later. They had seemed to think I was a spy or something and it took a bit to convince them that I had a contract with an Indian company to carry out a fishing survey of the two hundred nautical mile exclusive economic zone of the Andaman Islands.

Brian was satisfied with my qualifications and filled out the forms to confirm this to Peter; and then on to the boat. Brian got out his checklist and we immediately hit a problem. The very first check box on his form required the name of the vessel. For days it had been bothering me that the boat's name was not documented in any of her registration papers or on the vessel itself. There was no faded paintwork or filled holes to indicate the removal of a nameplate. No registration numbers. Nothing! It was a boat with no name, and this is unlucky.

I asked Peter for advice and he didn't think it was serious. We checked the registration booklet and there didn't seem to be a problem. She was indeed a current Hong Kong registered vessel; she had a number but no name. To avoid confusion we christened her in the name box *Technima 65*, which was her make and her model: an Italian-built, fibreglass, sixty-five foot luxury motor yacht. She had classical timeless lines and after twenty-two years could still mix it with style with much younger vessels.

"Okay young man, show me the engine room," said Brian, and we started with the inspection. The engines were all degreased and cleaned; the stainless steel floor plates were shining. Brian was very familiar with the main engines and knew that they were reliable workhorses. I told him of my diagnosis of the smoky starboard engine and he agreed, saying he would be interested to see what happened during the sea trials. We discussed the bilge system, fire-fighting abilities and fuel consumption, and he noted the two brand-new 24-volt banks of heavy-duty batteries in the lazaret. I operated the bilge pumps and fire pump in turn. Brian checked the seacocks, rudder stocks and exhaust outlets. He asked to hear and see the engine running and said he was looking for a minimum thirty pounds per square inch oil pressure at 1,500 rpms. I checked the oil and water and we headed to the bridge for the start up. Both engines fired instantly and we left them idling sweetly until they were warmed up.

There was a trace of a smile on Brian's face. Nothing sounds or feels much better (to an engineer) than the deep throb of a total of 2,400 brake horsepower. Once the temperature had reached eighty degrees I opened the throttles steadily until both engines had achieved a harmonic balance at 1,500 rpms. The deep throb turned into a powerful roar as the engines climbed to the cruising limits, the oil pressure held steady just under 50 psi – not the most I had seen but not the least; middle ground really. Brian agreed and added that if he took in the age and design of the engines it was not too bad at all, well above 30 psi. Checking the engine room, we couldn't say much over the din but noticed the manual pressure gauges attached directly to the engine blocks were reading just over 50 psi. Brian gave me the thumbs up. Back on the bridge I eased the throttles back, let the engines idle for a few minutes and shut them down. The engine room had passed inspection and Brian was satisfied that I had the skills to run it.

Next on the checklist were the navigation and communication equipment. The new radios were inspected and operated and communicated clearly with Hong Kong Port Control. The GPS plotter was noted and I explained that I was planning to back this unit up with the purchase of a complete set of paper charts, Admiralty sailing directions and associated equipment. The nav lights, compass lights and emergency lighting were all turned on and Brian checked the results. All were okay.

After Brian had finished with his paperwork we moved on to the safety and survival gear. He inspected what we had and ticked off the life raft, noting it had only a month left before it needed a service. I gave him the list of purchases I still needed to make and he accepted this on the condition that I sent him a copy of the itemised receipts for the articles I purchased as proof of this before we sailed. 'Before we sailed' – that was sounding positive. We did a walk around, checking the cabins, lifting all the floorboards to inspect the bilges. All was in order – everything was stored securely, the bilges dry. We finished up on the deck with Brian checking the deck fittings and anything else that he laid his eyes on. He checked the anchor, the chain and rope. I operated the anchor winch to his satisfaction, and then that was about it.

Back in the saloon Brian advised cheerfully that he had seen and heard enough and he would go back to his office to prepare a certificate of survey and a valuation report for Peter to consider for the insurance cover. Everybody was pleased with the results and Peter told me he would call to inform me as soon as the insurance was accepted. He told me that in the meantime he would liaise directly with Kurt and basically I could leave it all to him. He also informed me that part of his after sales service was to provide me with the assistance of one of his office staff in obtaining the necessary paperwork to export the vessel to Australia, and to go with me to customs and immigration for clearances. This was good news, which I was very grateful for. After all, this was communist China and communication and paperwork can be a nightmare to a novice. Satisfied, Brian handed me his bill. Ouch! $1,000 Australian. Not bad for three hours' work. I'm in the wrong business, I thought. But I didn't flinch; just smiled happily and told him I would deal with it immediately. I thanked them both for their help and time and after the arrival of a sampan, they were on their way with a goodbye wave.

"Good! Good! Good!" I said aloud, as I relaxed into the leather settee in the saloon. It had been a good morning; the survey had passed with flying colours, my tickets and experience had been accepted and there was the added bonus of networking in the super yacht or white boat industry. Everything was running smoothly and after tomorrow's sea trials the countdown would be on.

Apart from all the operational checks I had to calculate my fuel consumption as accurately as possible. The only practical way to do this was to empty the day or service tank, close the fuel transfer valves and then refill the day tank with a measured amount of fuel, and then record the time and speed it took to run empty. I was busy with this task in the engine room when I heard Steve and Malan jump on board. I went up to greet them and they were both as happy as. Surrounded by piles of shopping bags, they had had a good day. I told Steve about the survey and he was rapt. I helped them on board with their shopping bags, full of heaps of food, drinks and all sorts of delicacies and goodies for the following day's sea trials. I had asked Florida and Malan if they would like to bring some friends to be our guests during the sea trials and the invitation had been enthusiastically accepted, with Florida offering to do the catering for us. A day spent cruising the islands of Hong Kong in a super yacht was looking good in my mind. I left Steve and Malan to sort everything out and went back to the engine room to finish working on the day tank.

I awoke to a glorious morning, sunny, and with not a breath of wind or a cloud in sight. It was a perfect day for sea trials. The sea was flat calm which was good – it would greatly reduce the chances of anyone's day being spoilt by the dreaded curse of seasickness. I made my way to the bathroom to shower, shave and dress. Today I was going to act and dress like the captain of a super yacht because that is what I was, even if it was just for the day. I was going to enjoy myself. I took my time and emerged on deck a while later in pressed black trousers with belt buckle shining, a crisp white shirt, polished black deck shoes and a pair of Armani (fake!) sunglasses and a navy blue cap.

"Bloody oath, that's the go, Skip!" Steve was most impressed with my look and he was looking pretty sharp too. He had good taste and a body to go with it; a more youthful look than mine, casual and tropical. His purchases yesterday suited the day perfectly. Malan appeared in the saloon. She had stayed the night and damned if she didn't look just beautiful, the shopping spree yesterday paying handsome dividends.

Eddy turned up on schedule and soon we were busy preparing the vessel to get underway. I asked Eddy if he would have a quick dive and check for any hull fouling, especially around the two propellers and rudders. The boat had been sitting at her mooring for quite a while and the anchorage was a tangle of lines going in all directions. It was quite possible that a rope might be snagged somewhere. Steve supervised Eddy in the water and I went to the bridge and removed the ignition keys and turned the master switch off. Nobody could start the motors and engage the gearboxes until Eddy was safely out of the water.

Malan was already busy in the galley so I went down to the engine room to do my final inspections. I checked the dipsticks and the coolant levels and opened the seacocks, all the time looking for items that were out of place or not secured or lashed down. I lifted the inspection cover over the day tank to see if the fuel level was where I had left it yesterday, and it was. Everything was in order. Steve had done a good job in the lazaret. All spares, drums and tools were expertly lashed down and secured. The emergency tiller had been made ready for use and was locked in its holding cradle.

Back on the bridge the fuel gauges were reading a bit over a third full on both tanks, maybe a bit over 2,000 litres, sufficient for the day. In general, I don't trust electric fuel gauges so I checked the tanks manually from their filler positions on the side decks. They showed over 1,000 litres a side. While on the deck I also made the anchor ready for instantly letting go. Eddy was happily sitting back in his dinghy, water trickling down his tanned and compact body. He called out, "All okay, Captain! Your hull is clean and no obstructions."

"Thanks Eddy," I replied. Eddy went off on his daily rounds and wished us a successful day while Steve and I busied ourselves shortening up the lines, leaving two bow and two stern lines holding us in position. We had just finished doing this when an overloaded sampan appeared, heading straight for us. It was Florida and her friends.

Bloody oath, this was turning out to be a beauty parade and a fashion show. Like Malan, Florida and her friends were all decked out in style. Florida beamed at me from under a large, white sun hat. Funny, I thought to myself, looks can be deceiving. Today nobody could tell that these six poor ladies who shared a tiny, two-bedroom flat in Hong Kong and two equally broke fishermen were not the real thing when it comes to super yachts, the rich and famous! Florida ushered the girls inside to show them around and told me I would find her in the galley.

"Okay, let's get this show on the road," I said to Steve. I started the engines and monitored their warm-up while Steve checked the engine room. I settled myself with the fly bridge controls. This was going to be a new experience, a planing hull with twin 1,000 horsepower plus engines. I had spent my entire career in displacement hulls with single shafts but I prided myself in my ship handling abilities and was confident I could handle my charge. Still tied fast, I gently engaged forward and reverse gears in turn, feeling the vessel surge under my commands. Satisfied, I called down to Steve who was ready on deck, "Let her all go mate!"

Within a few minutes we were clear of the breakwater and had entered the island-strewn South China Sea. I went straight into my first task, monitoring the fuel consumption. I left the fly bridge and turned to the bridge, noted the trim, and gently eased the throttles open. A tremor went through the boat as she started surging forward from 700 rpm at idle to 800, 900 then 1,000 rpm. I had my eyes glued to the GPS screen and the speed-over-ground readout in particular. Speed over ground, or SOG, is the best way to measure distance as the alternative speed over water doesn't allow for current or drift and can lead to false readings and incorrect calculations. The black LED numbers started to rise – five knots, six knots, seven knots, eight, eight point four knots, eight point eight, eight point nine, and then steadied. I inched the throttles forward to 1,100 revs per minute. Nine knots, nine point five, nine point six, nine point seven, nine point eight; and settled again. I was happy. I was very close to my estimated ten knots with the engines only lightly loaded.

I noted the time again. My plan was to box the compass in fifteen minute legs: fifteen minutes to the west, fifteen minutes to the north; then to the east and then to the south. I figured this would nullify the effects of any unknown current and drift on my speed. As I was navigating the square, Steve was downstairs; earmuffs on, monitoring the fuel flow and engine room in general. Around we went, arriving back at my starting position exactly one hour later.

The speed-over-ground indicator varied slightly between nine point six and ten point one knots.

Steve came up from the engine room and said he thought the fuel level was only halfway towards the mark I had made in the tank. This sounded good so far. I decided to do another lap to confirm our calculations and around we went again. An hour later we were finished and I was able to carry out my fuel calculations. I would have more than enough reserves to make the first leg of five hundred nautical miles. I smiled to myself; how close had I been to my initial calculations?

During this time I had been monitoring the engine gauges and all the other equipment on the bridge. Everything was within its operational limits and the electrical system was all in the green. Steve reported that all the bilges were dry. Nothing had gone amiss so far. I headed the boat towards a group of islands I had spotted earlier. We would go and 'discover' the islands, find a place to test the anchor and have lunch. "Here you go Steve, get a feel for her." He happily propped himself in the helm chair and took over the con.

"Feels sweet, eh Skip?" I agreed. The motors were working just enough and were gently throbbing away and we were getting through the water easily. Not quite planing, but semi-planing, we had a small trim to the stern but not uncomfortably so. The girls were thoroughly enjoying themselves, lounging about, chatting on the cream leather sofas or helping Florida in the galley. Malan had joined Steve on the double leather seat of the helm and was happily nestled in as he steered us on our course. I didn't have to ask him if he had everything under control.

I decided to check on the rest of our guests, never allowing the sound or motion of the boat to leave my senses. Florida, as expected, was immersed in the galley with happy, chatting helpers all around her. I knew better than to interfere in this department and just called out, "Everybody okay down there?" A chorus of happy affirmatives answered me back.

I wandered out to the aft deck and noticed the white smoke of the starboard engine had definitely cleared a bit. I stood for a while, mesmerised by the wake throwing out from the stern, looking at the pattern of bubbles caused by the two propellers spinning relentlessly below the hull. I walked around the deck, stopping at the bow. It was quiet up here. I could hardly hear the engines, just the slapping of water on the bow as we cut through a tiny slop. Resting on the side rails I watched as we drew near the island. The first way point I had punched into the plotter for anchoring was close but not good enough. Before long I had found an ideal spot, a small cove in the lee of one of the small islands, complete with a white sandy beach fringed by lush tropical greenery. It was perfect. After a cautious approach I could see the sandy bottom and we dropped the pick.

What a spread it was. This time Florida and her helpers had really outdone themselves. It was a veritable banquet of Asian flavours. For the next couple of hours we simply enjoyed ourselves. It was idyllic – the cove, the boat and the companions.

It was with some regret that I eventually started the motors to head back to Hong Kong and set the course back home. Florida joined me in the fly bridge and we sat together as

I steered across the ocean. One last test, a run under full load; if the motors couldn't handle that then they would be no good to me at all. I had been waiting for this moment all day. Slowly, but without stopping, I pushed the throttles to their stops. The steady beat of the motors and motion of the boat that we were used to suddenly changed. With a deep roar increasing in intensity every second as the motors wound up, the boat surged forward and onto the plane, levelling off nicely. Wow! This felt good. It was totally smooth out of the water, and the steering was light and responsive. This was what she was built for, dashing around the bays and waterways of the world's exotica. With the wind in our faces, Florida cuddled up next to me as we blasted toward Hong Kong at close to twenty knots, the twin ten-inch exhausts singing their tune as they expelled 2,500 horsepower from the bowels of the boat. In no time we were across the stretch of water and I eased the throttles back as we idled around the waterways of Hong Kong. I spotted a bay with half a dozen super yachts at anchor and thought, why not? I safely anchored clean in the middle of them and we were soon enjoying coffee and snacks on the aft deck – afternoon tea you might say. It was a little amusing to receive and return the happy waves from the 'other' rich and famous.

The sun was getting low and I had achieved my aims – a satisfactory sea trial and an absolutely fantastic day. Steve pulled the anchor and I turned the boat for home. We were safely moored with all lines secured without a bump or scratch just as the sun set. All the girls agreed that they had had a wonderful time, that it had been a special day in their lives. I received a much longer kiss and hug from Florida than previously and we agreed to meet the following day for some shopping and a meal – just the two of us.

Eddy and the engineer from the yard turned up bright and early a bit after 0700 hours with three one-cubic metre fuel tanks and a couple of helpers. Steve and I helped manhandle the fuel tanks into place on the aft deck. This was going to be three tons of fuel that we would carry, quite a weight for the deck, not to mention the changes it would make to the stability calculations. I decided to secure the tanks as far forward as I could, and selected a position directly over the engine room lazaret bulkhead where there was maximum hull strength. This cramped our access to the saloon quite a bit but it was the best place for them. I could still freely access the lazaret hatch and the locker holding the life raft. I then helped with the fuel transfer. Before long I had a fuel hose attached and the pump was running until the boat's fuel tanks were chock-a-block, holding close to 7,300 litres and a short time later another 3,000 litres had been added to the on-deck tanks.

After finishing with the fuel we hailed a sampan and were off to complete our shopping. I called Kurt on the way across the harbour, and he was rapt with the sea trial results. He told me he had organised the insurance with Peter and that the paperwork would be available by the end of the day. We were both excited. There was no foreseeable reason why we could not sail the following day, only one day behind schedule.

We both had our reasons for wanting to be home by Christmas. For me it was my family. It had literally been decades since the Smith family had been together on Christmas Day. It had been arranged months and months ago. My father and mother, their seven children and nineteen grandchildren were getting together at our family home at Naracoorte, a small country town in the south east of South Australia. It was going to be a big, happy and joyous reunion. My father, a retired country surgeon who had dedicated his life to the care of the community, and my mother, his beloved wife, were over the moon at the prospect of having all of us safely under the one roof; the same roof we all grew up under. I can remember Dad saying to me during the planning that it would be maybe for the last time. I was determined not to let them down.

I paid the sampan lady and we jumped ashore on the island that I had visited earlier with Eddy and began the shopping. We went from shop to shop, ticking off the list as we went. Pumps, hoses, cable ties, life rings, duct tape, electronic tape, tools, torches, batteries, strobe lights, buckets, fire extinguishers, flares, whistles, electrical fittings, CRC grease shackles, rope and more. I came to the last item, the EPIRB. After enquiring at a few different shops I had run into a dilemma. EPIRBs come in two basic types, one with a 121.5 MHz transponder and the other a 406 MHz transponder. The 121.5 MHz EPIRB was the earlier type and relied on low-orbit satellites and civilian aircraft to receive the distress signal. It covered all coastal waters but not the deep oceans. I had studied the footprints of the available satellites and had worked out that, give or take a few miles, the 121.5 MHz model would give us adequate coverage. We had the aircraft as a backup. It was by far cheaper, a few hundred dollars compared with the 406 at a few thousand dollars. They were, however, being phased out to be replaced globally by the 406 MHz model. These were more powerful units with more features, using geostationary satellites and pretty much foolproof. Once activated, the ship in distress would be immediately identified and its position plotted. This would automatically initiate a global search and rescue operation linked to the GMDSS system that was also entering general service. With the 406 it was a matter of switching it on and waiting patiently to be rescued. My dilemma was that the 121.5 MHz Empire had already been phased out in Hong Kong and was not available. Anybody can buy a 121.5 off the shelf and go back to their boat and mount it, but not so the 406. It had to be fitted by a certified technician and a host of registration, ownership and identification paperwork had to be lodged with the relevant country and global authorities. With this extra cost and the time delay I made a big mistake. I guiltily crossed EPIRB off the list. I still had lots to do and besides, I had carried an EPIRB for the past fifteen years and had never switched one on.

We bundled ourselves into a taxi and made our way back to Aberdeen and the boat. On our trip back, Peter called and told me that the insurance and export paperwork had been finished and that he would send his assistant to the boat first thing in the morning to take me where I had to go. After thanking him and hanging up I said to Steve, "It's all good mate. Unless we can think of anything that we have forgotten we are ready to throw the ropes."

I told him I was going to clean up and spend the afternoon and evening with Florida. He had decided to do the same with Malan. We were going to be in each other's faces for the next few days so spending a night apart wasn't a bad idea.

Exactly one hour later I was leaning against the sea wall in Aberdeen. A few minutes passed then Florida rushed at me with hugs and kisses. We walked off into the city hand in hand, as natural as a happily married couple. I was famished so we decided to find something to eat. There were literally hundreds of small eateries selling all sorts of Oriental foods, their aromas filling the streets. Florida selected one and over freshly made and cooked noodles, we chatted away, making our plans for the afternoon. I wanted to do a heap of Christmas shopping and after explaining what I was looking for, Florida decided on the Chinese market. I was really enjoying Florida's company; she was always happy, straightforward, honest and caring. Not to mention her beguiling Asian good looks. Conversation was not hard.

After lunch we caught a taxi and made our way to the market. There were acres of cavernous buildings filled with thousand of stalls selling just about everything imaginable. I said to Florida firmly, "Now don't you go and lose me in this place, please. We will never find each other again."

"I will never lose you," she proclaimed, as she grabbed my hand firmly and led the way. Up and down and around we went. There were bargains to be had: a dive watch and carved chess set for Daniel, souvenirs for the family; and clothes, clothes, clothes. Sophie was into clothes and with Florida's good taste, I soon had an armful. Every time I noticed that something had caught Florida's eye, I would wait until her attention was focused elsewhere and sneak back and buy it.

A few hours later we were finished, literally. We did not have room on our fingers for one more bag. We decided to head back to the boat with our loot and start afresh. When we made it back, Steve was not around. Good. We had the night and the boat to ourselves. We took the shopping below to my cabin and went through it all, packing it safely away. When we were nearly finished I took one of the bags and handed it to Florida. "This is for you as thanks for all you have done for me; the cooking, the cleaning, shopping and your friendship," I said.

She looked inside and saw what I had bought. She was still looking down when she quietly said, "Nobody has ever bought me so many beautiful things. Thank you, you are too kind." She reached up and gave me a big hug, but not before I noticed a single tear running down her cheek. I held her until I figured it had dried and said, "Let's wash this city grime off and go out and enjoy ourselves."

"Me first," she announced as she calmly and unashamedly undressed down to nothing and stepped into the bathroom. She was back to her normal happy self. Florida was definitely getting to me. When she reappeared, I nearly dropped my coffee on my new spotless charts. Beautiful, radiant, gorgeous, raced through my mind. "You look absolutely smashing," I managed to say. She just smiled, making her even more attractive.

We decided on the Wan Chai district where there was plenty to eat, see and do and stood arm in arm at the stern of the boat waiting for a sampan. We had a great night. A long dinner at a classy Japanese restaurant, dancing off the food to a live band in a crowded, boisterous night club and finishing up in a quiet bar sipping cocktails; all the while getting to know each other better and better. We spoke of our families, our lives and our dreams. Before we knew it, it was the pumpkin hour; time for the last sampan. Florida took my hands and looked straight into my eyes and said, "I want to stay with you tonight."

There was no escaping the morning. I was entwined as one with Florida and lay there waiting for my dreams to fade and thinking of the coming day – D-day, departure day. I always get the same feeling when I am about to leave for the sea; excitement about the challenges and the unknown that lies ahead. But also sadness for those I must leave behind. It gives me a knot in my stomach. I turned my head and looked at Florida peacefully sleeping. We hadn't spoken a word on the subject and had acted as if this day would never come. The knot pulled even tighter. I can never work out why I just go and leave all the people I love, or in Florida's case, a very special person who had suddenly come into my life. I consoled myself by knowing that I would keep in touch. Who knows what the future held for us? Florida stirred and opened her eyes. "Good morning, sweetheart," she purred, and snuggled even closer. There was no rushing this morning. Damn, it was going to be hard to say goodbye.

Eventually and like a reluctant tiger, I made my way to the shower to start the day.

Steve and I were busy discussing the day's plan and Florida was helping clean up after breakfast when there was a familiar nudge at the stern. Peter's assistant had arrived, a smartly dressed Chinese lady who introduced herself as Annie. I sat down with her to discuss the course of action. First it was off to the Hong Kong ships registry office, next to customs, and finally immigration. Annie said if we made an early start we would be finished by lunchtime.

Over breakfast Steve and Florida had agreed to do the food shopping and Steve was going to top up the fresh water tanks and double check that everything on board was secure and shipshape. The first leg was a short hop of approximately five hundred nautical miles, so we only needed three days' supply of food. The only system that was not operational on board was the domestic refrigeration and air conditioning plant. I had checked earlier in the week and it was totally kaput – a seized electric motor and compressors. No gas, no go. It was not a vital system and I could easily live without it. But I asked Steve to add two ice boxes and some ice to his list. We could store them on the back deck where they could drain. Not entirely trusting the Hong Kong water supply and for safety reasons, I also asked him to buy at least a dozen two litre bottles of purified water. With all this settled we agreed to meet at lunchtime.

Annie was a great help. I quickly realised that there was no way I could have done without her assistance. This was communist China and officialdom was the order of the day.

Sitting in my chair in the waiting room, I let Annie do the talking. Paper after paper was scrutinised, checked and discussed, then taken somewhere else to be checked again. It was with some relief when I saw the stamp pad finally opening in the different offices. Between stops, while patiently waiting for our number to come up, Annie and I chatted away. She kept on repeating how brave we were to be taking 'that boat' to Australia. Not 'that small boat' and not 'that old boat', just 'that boat'. I kept on telling her that Steve and I had plenty of experience and it wasn't that much of a big deal, really. But Annie's references to 'that boat' did strike me as a bit odd. After what seemed an age, Annie announced that everything was in order and we could make our way to immigration. We were quickly given clearances to depart Hong Kong in a boat with no name.

The stamps on our passport showed that I had twenty-four hours in which to depart. Not a minute too soon, I thought, as I looked at the sky. I had been closely following the weather reports all week in the newspapers and on the television and radio. The monsoon was definitely coming and the signs were visible. In contrast to the warm, clear and windless days of the past week, a change was in the air. The temperature had dropped but more significantly, a steady wind was blowing from the north-east. High altitude, wispy clouds were beginning to appear overhead. There was no reason to panic. We would still be all right if we left in the next few hours. I figured I would be steering away from the head of the storm and within fifty hours or so I would be running tucked nice and close in the lee of the Philippines. I sniffed the wind. Maybe fifteen to twenty knots max, I decided. Still time enough.

After bidding farewell to Annie and clutching our passports tightly, I jumped into a cab to take me back to Aberdeen and the boat. Before catching a sampan I stopped at the boatyard to pay the accounts and thank everybody for their help. While the bill was being made up, a rather serious looking secretary looked over at me and said, "So you are the one taking that boat to Australia?" There it was again, 'that boat'. On the way down to catch a sampan, 'that boat, that boat' was ringing in my brain.

Florida and Steve were on board when I arrived, busy stowing the food and drinks. Besides the water, Steve had bought fruit juice, milk and soft drinks; plenty of liquids. I placed the passports on the table and said, "We are free to depart. All done."

It was about 1300 hours so I still had a couple of hours up my sleeve. "Would you like to come with me to Aberdeen to do some last-minute shopping and have a bit of lunch?" I asked Florida. We left Steve doing his rounds. He still had the fresh water tanks to fill.

Florida and I made our way across the harbour. I didn't really need to do any shopping; it was just an excuse to spend the last few hours with her. We tried hard to be happy but there was an overriding sense of sadness as we wandered aimlessly around the city. We stopped for lunch in a tiny restaurant in one of the crowded streets. I told Florida that I would call her as soon as I got to the Philippines in a few days' time to let her know that we were safe. In fact, I told her that I would call her at every port in our voyage. I also told her that even though I had only known her for seven short days I thought she was a beautiful lady, inside and out, and that I would so much like to keep in touch when I returned home to Australia. She smiled and replied, "I think the same of you. Let's please stay in touch."

We walked to the bus stop hand in hand in silence. Florida bowed her head, trying to hide the tears I knew were running down her face. Her bus was waiting. She pressed a piece of paper into my hands – her address and contact numbers in the Philippines. I placed them safely in my wallet. We looked at each other for a few seconds. Even with all the tears she still looked beautiful. We kissed one last time and I turned and left. Not only did I have a knot in my stomach but a big lump in my throat. At the underpass to the waterfront I glanced back. The bus had left but Florida was still sitting at the bus stop, her head lowered, both hands clutching a white handkerchief to her face. I didn't know it then but I was never going to see her again. Her address and phone number are lost forever, along with my wallet and cell phone, lying on the seabed for eternity in the still, inky blackness.

We were finally ready to depart. Steve went to the engine room to monitor the warm up and I hit the keys. The engines quickly settled into their by then familiar rumble. I busied myself selecting the first chart. Steve had already laid them out in their correct sequence. I knew I could rely on him: a strong, reliable and experienced seaman. Next I called Hong Kong Port Control VHF and asked for permission to depart and gave them my destination. It was Manila in the Philippines. "*Technima 65*, you are cleared for departure. Have a safe voyage," came the reply.

Steve came up and gave the thumbs up. "All okay down there Skip," he said.

"All right, throw the ropes. Let's blow this joint." I wove my way carefully down the line of boats and a few minutes later we cleared the breakwater. The sun was just beginning to set so it was on with the nav lights, which Steve checked and they were all burning bright. I noted the time, date and position in the log book and eased the throttle to 1,100 revs per minute and watched as the black LED readout of speed over ground on the GPS unit steadied a few minutes later at 9.5 knots. We were on our way.

The Sinking

It was 1800 hours when I cleared the breakwater of Aberdeen. In order to set a course for the Philippines I had to first clear Hong Kong and the outlying islands of Dang Gang Lidao, some fifteen nautical miles to the south of Hong Kong. The first leg took in the shipping channel and, after a series of doglegs, the open sea.

We steamed away from land and entered the shipping channel, turning south. Hong Kong has one of the busiest shipping concentrations in the world. I passed dozens and dozens of ships, incoming and outgoing, of all shapes and sizes – coastal tramps, barges, tugs, car carriers, bulk carriers, container vessels and monster crude oil carriers, all purposefully going about their business. I stayed out of the way by hugging the starboard side of the channel. Without radar and steering by hand, I could do only one thing. Concentrate. I said to Steve, "Have a quick look around and grab a bit of sleep. I will do the first watch and you can do the next one. I'll get you up around midnight." Before heading to his bunk he reported back that everything was shipshape.

On the dash, all the gauges and indicators were in the green; she was running sweet and we were doing just a fraction under ten knots. We were off to a good start. I bade Florida a silent farewell and was looking forward to calling her in a few days' time. But I was back in my element. A lonely nightshift was part of my life. I felt at ease, confident of what I was doing.

Three hours later I cleared the outlying islands and set the course for the Philippines – a straight-line run of four hundred and fifty nautical miles – approximately fifty hours to go. The wind had definitely picked up now, twenty to twenty-five knots and steady from the north-east, and was kicking up a two to three metre sea. The cloud cover had thickened and we were rolling a bit, but still had the weather aft of the beam where I liked it – not perfect conditions but I had learnt long ago that at sea, you had to take the good with the bad. We were still making steady progress at around 7.9 knots at 1,100 revs per minute. The stars had all disappeared behind the clouds so I had to steer by the compass and by feel, keeping the sea on my stern quarter. I steamed through the darkness in a semi-trance-like state, as I concentrated on the compass and made small automatic corrections to the helm with every movement of the boat.

Steve appeared on cue at midnight, rubbing the sleep out of his eyes, and after getting himself a cup of coffee, took up position behind the helm. I checked the paper charts one last time while he settled himself in. Once I was satisfied that everything was under control I said, "It's a straight run now to the Philippines. Just keep her on this course and I'll see you in the morning."

I headed to my cabin and jumped into bed. Sleep comes easily to me when underway and the motion of the boat rocked me quickly into dreamland. Some time later, I awoke abruptly from a deep sleep and checked my watch. It was 6 a.m. For some reason I don't understand, I have an inbuilt alarm and can wake myself to the minute, no matter how tired I am. It never ceases to amaze me. I dressed and made my way to the bridge and a few minutes later I was at the wheel. "I'll take it until midday. Go get yourself a good sleep, mate," I said to Steve. He wasted no time in going down, with assurances he would be up at twelve o'clock.

The day broke grey and sombre. The barometer had fallen a few points overnight, which meant that the wind would increase. As long as it kept coming from the same direction it would be okay. A few minutes before midday Steve appeared and took over. After six hours behind the wheel I was ready for a break and gladly handed over to him. It's not too bad steering in daylight because you can see the run of the sea. All you have to do is keep it at a constant angle to the boat and you're pretty much on course. It's far easier than chasing the compass with no visible horizon at night.

After handing over the helm to Steve, I went to the engine room to check on things there. Everything looked good. The motors were beating a steady rhythm, the 240-volt generator was chugging away normally and the bilges were dry.

I was starving. I hadn't eaten since lunchtime yesterday, so I went down to the galley and returned soon after with two plates of eggs, bacon, baked beans, toast and a jug of orange juice.

"Get this into yourself," I said to Steve, handing him a plate.

"Just what the doctor ordered," said Steve, getting stuck into the food.

"That feels better," I said a few minutes later, wiping my plate clean. "You okay here for a few hours?"

"No worries mate," he replied.

With that, I went downstairs and collapsed on my bunk, and was instantly asleep.

Suddenly I was wide-awake. Something had woken me and I was on full alert. A quick glance at my watch told me it was 1300 hours. Why was I awake? I still had five hours of sleep to go. I listened to the boat and there it was, a variation in the revs of one of the main engines. I lay there for a minute, listening, hoping the problem would clear itself. A list of probable causes went through my mind: fuel starvation, maybe an air block, clogged air filters, or a problem in the throttle control cables and junction boxes. It could have been any number of things.

Suddenly, it got worse. I leapt out of bed, threw on my clothes and dashed upstairs, meeting Steve halfway. "I think we have a problem, Skip," he said as we quickly made our way to the bridge.

The revs on the starboard motor were fluctuating wildly, the needle on the gauge rising and falling between 1,100 and 1,500 revs per minute. I quickly scanned down the gauges – oil pressure okay, water temperature okay, oil temperature okay, and alternator okay. But when I came to the last one, the gearbox oil pressure, the needle was in its resting place, on zero. I pulled both throttles back to idle and slipped the starboard engine into neutral. "Steer her the best you can downwind for a while. I'm going to the engine room," I told Steve.

In the engine room there was oil everywhere, covering the starboard gearbox and shaft and splattered all over the bulkheads, ceiling and floor. I knew immediately what had happened. The rear end gearbox seal had blown. I cursed and made my way to the lazaret. Unlashing a drum of gear oil from the store, I grabbed a funnel and some rags and started adding oil to the damaged gearbox, but it was useless. As fast as I could pour it in the oil ran out of the shattered seal. Damn! This is what happens to boats that just lie around without proper care or maintenance. The seal had dried and cracked and corrosion had set in, chewing out the rubber seal like a hacksaw through butter. Eddy would have started the motors every couple of weeks but he never would have given the gearboxes a run. This was bad enough for the engines, let alone the boxes. I cursed this universal lack of knowledge and respect for machinery. There was absolutely nothing I could do. I was down to one engine plain and simple. The starboard shaft was freewheeling because of the water flowing through the propeller. I had to stop this, otherwise it would cause more damage to the gearbox.

I gathered up rope, packing timbers and wedges from the lazaret and set about the task. It is not easy to stop a spinning, oily stainless steel shaft weighing half a ton or more but I persevered, getting covered in oil until I got the job done. I mopped up the mess as best I could and made my way back to the bridge. I had some decisions to make.

"The gearbox is fucked," I said to Steve as I shut down the starboard engine. "No point in wasting fuel."

"Shit," was about all he could reply.

Okay. Where was I and what was I going to do? I manipulated the controls on the GPS plotter and blew the chart up to a large scale. Hong Kong was one hundred and fifty nautical miles behind us and Manila in the Philippines was four hundred nautical miles ahead. I swung the boat about on our previous course and opened the port throttle to 1,100 revs per minute. The boat was hard to handle but the speed over ground remained steady at 5.8 knots. On only one engine, I still had enough fuel to make it as far as the Philippines and I didn't want to give up on the voyage yet. I could replace the seal in Manila and continue on our way. This would put us behind schedule but even if I could get the boat as far as Port Moresby or Lae in New Guinea, or even Cairns in Australia, I could fly home for Christmas and finish the delivery afterwards. And anyway, I needed the money.

The thought of punching our way back to Hong Kong in worsening weather didn't seem like much of an option. The situation was serious but not uncommon or life threatening. The rest of the boat was functioning normally. On the other hand, Hong Kong was the closest and safest choice. What if the other gearbox seal failed? I decided to keep on heading towards the Philippines while I thought about what to do, but the decision was taken out of my hands and made for me, because I could not keep the boat on course.

With the weather pushing the bow to starboard and the port side propeller doing the same, the boat just wanted to turn to starboard; the helm had no effect. Even hard to port the boat continued relentlessly the other way. I tried increasing the revs to see if I could get more water flow over the rudders to give them more bite, but it didn't make any difference. It didn't matter how I manipulated the throttle or the helm, I could not maintain my heading. So I had no choice in the matter. I let the boat swing to starboard until we were on a reciprocal course heading back to Hong Kong, where we would just have to start our trip over again.

Travelling in this direction, the weather and the port side propulsion cancelled each other out and with careful helm movements I was able to maintain a constant heading in the direction of land. Our speed was down to 4.5 knots as we punched and slogged our way into deteriorating weather. It was going to take twenty-four hours or more before we were safely back in Hong Kong. "Sorry mate, but the show's over for us for the moment," I had to inform Steve. "We'll get back to Hong Kong and make a fresh start."

I didn't believe we were in serious danger but I was bitterly disappointed. But there was no point crying over spilt milk; what had happened had happened. I went over everything I had done to prepare the boat and reassured myself that

I could not have foreseen the damaged seal. It was simply a case of returning to Hong Kong and supervising the repairs. At least Florida would be happy, even though I hated returning with my tail between my legs.

It was 1400 hours on the 6th of December and my position was 20° 42′ North and 115° 45′ East when we started our slow and uncomfortable journey back to Hong Kong. By then the wind had built up to thirty knots and was gusting higher, still steady from the north-east, maybe backing to the east a fraction. The cloud cover was complete and lowering, the waves had risen to a nasty four to five metre sea with white caps and broken seas all round. This was going to be a crap twenty-four hours or so. I had been in plenty of big seas before and all you can do is grin and bear it.

I asked Steve to do a thorough inspection of the boat, inside and out, to check that everything was secure and that we would have no further problems. I concentrated on keeping the boat heading in the right direction, cursing that little piece of cheap rubber that had let us down.

Steve completed his rounds and told me he had double lashed the fuel containers on the aft deck and that everything else was in order. Well, twenty-four hours of shit and we would be tied up safely in Aberdeen Harbour. Steve made up some sandwiches and coffee, which we ate gloomily on the bridge as we painfully and slowly headed back towards land. I told Steve to go and get some rest and that I'd call him in a few hours time to take over. We were not at all fazed by the situation, we had both experienced plenty of breakdowns at sea and this was just another one. Steve's last comment before he left for his bunk was, "Ah well, mate. Not to worry, it's not your fault. Anyway, it will be good to see the girls again."

It was very uncomfortable with the boat rolling and pitching heavily, with nerve-wracking clangs and crashes as items were thrown around in their lockers. There were sounds reverberating throughout the boat. It was close to 1500 hours when I heard a more distinct, heavy smashing sound coming from the engine room. What the hell was that? Steve had heard it too and was up in a flash. I handed him the helm and went to investigate.

The watertight engine room door had come adrift in the pounding and was smashing into the damaged starboard gearbox. I grabbed it and tried to secure the locks but couldn't, and a quick inspection showed me why. The bottom locking arm was bent at a forty-five degree angle as a result of its slamming into the solid steel mass of the gearbox. And even worse, the bent arm had twisted the guide rails and jammed the entire locking system. What next? This was a workshop job. I didn't want to lash the door half closed – I might have to get to the engine room in a hurry. So I secured it hard up against the offending gearbox, which was the best I could do for the time being.

Shit happens, I told myself as I returned to the bridge. I filled Steve in, with his only comment being, "Fucking weather." Steve was happy to sit up for a while and said he would call me in a few hours' time. It had been a long day and I gratefully headed for my cabin.

The boat was rolling heavily and sleep didn't come easily. I was tossing around on my bed deciding whether to get up or not when, close to 1800 hours, I felt a totally different motion of the boat. As we rolled down the side of a big sea, the boat seemed to stagger and hold as she struggled to regain her normal trim in the water. It didn't feel good and a tiny chill raced down my spine. I was up in a flash and raced to the bridge. Steve had also felt it but he had other problems to deal with. The dashboard was going crazy, red lights were flashing everywhere.

"Quick Steve, check the engine room!"

As he rushed off, another big wave hit us, causing the same motion as before, only worse. I heard Steve groan at the bottom of the stairs leading to my cabin and the engine room and in the same instant, I realised that we were down by the stern, with the bow clearly rising. "You had better have a look mate," Steve called. "I'm going to unstow the life raft."

I raced down the stairs. Holy shit, the engine room was flooding, and the lazaret as well, at an incredible rate. The sea just seemed to be welling up through the boat. The electric bilge pumps were already under water and totally useless. My first reaction was to attempt to operate the valve on the remaining engine, to suck water from the engine room and discharge it overboard. I knelt down, up to my chest in water, and reached down under the motor to operate the valve and let out a shriek of pain. Not being able to see what I was doing and working by feel, I had stuck my thumb between a vee belt and a spinning pulley. On the second attempt I opened the valve but absolutely nothing happened. I was losing her, no question about it. The water was by now chest high; it was climbing the stairs nearly as fast as I was. I had only seconds to make preparations to abandon ship.

Adrenalin flowing through me, at the top of the stairs I shouted out to Steve, "Launch the life raft and grab as much food and water as you can! Don't forget the flares!" I raced to the SSB radio. I had preset it to 6215 megahertz – a long-range international distress frequency. There was no time to reset it to the more preferred 2182 MHz. I grabbed the mike, took a deep breath and pushed the transmit button.

"Mayday! Mayday! Mayday! This is *Technima 65*, my position is 20° 57′ North 115° 38′ East! We are two souls on board! We are sinking and we're preparing to abandon ship! We need urgent assistance!" I then repeated the message. Over the static I heard the familiar sound of clicking as if someone had heard my call and was trying to reply, but I couldn't be sure. Then the radio went dead. In fact, the whole boat went dead. I grabbed a half-full bottle of water, a torch and the hand-held VHF radio, and made my way aft, grabbing a couple of packets of lollies, a chocolate bar and a tin of peanuts from the bar in the saloon as I went. She was going fast, the deck was at a crazy angle as the stern sunk to meet the sea. Steve had the deflated raft in the water and was pulling frantically on the painter cord. After a few agonising seconds the sound of high-pressure air reached our ears and the life raft exploded into being. In the next few seconds we threw everything we could into the life raft – bottles of water, juice, milk, soft drinks, fruit, a block of cheese, along with the flares and the few things I had gathered on the way out. I thought of going back inside for one more gathering mission but it was out of the question; she was nearly gone, and being stuck inside a sinking boat would not be a good way to go.

"Okay Steve, jump in!" I said as I held the raft close. He was in and then it was my turn. I untied the painter holding us to the sinking boat and jumped into the raft. From when I had left my cabin to when I jumped into the life raft had taken about sixty seconds.

Day 1
Stripped Bare

"We are alright," I said to Steve as we looked at each other with concern; puzzlement, fear and confusion on our faces.

"Shit that was quick," Steve muttered.

I opened the flaps on the canopy and looked outside. The yacht was sliding backwards into the ocean. I could see the fly bridge, superstructure and targa arch breaking apart as they hit the sea. There was a massive explosion of air and bubbles as the saloon and the bridge succumbed to the waves with one mighty inrush of water. She sat perfectly upright for a few minutes, just the bow pointing to the heavens until the fo'c'sle watertight door gave way and she slid out of sight; our home, our haven, taken from us in minutes. We were abandoned in the sea in a tiny square of rubber tubing. Steve poked his head out and together we scanned for anything that may have floated free and could help us, but there was nothing of use to be had. The raft was already fifty metres from the flotsam and moving further away every second. We were being moved by the wind, while everything else was drifting in the current. After searching for a few more minutes, there was nothing more to be seen. There was just us in the raft and the ocean. Night was setting in and the storm was intensifying and we were being bounced around in the life raft like a couple of drunks.

The canvas bag, complete with zipper, that the life raft had been packed in was still attached to the raft with a short painter line and I dragged it in. Over the years Steve and I had attended many survival courses held at the Australian Maritime College and had a good idea of the life raft drill. Deploy the sea anchor, sponge out the interior of the raft, take an inventory of every item on board, check the raft for damage and correct inflation, inflate the double bottom if cold and take a seasick pill whether you liked it or not; and finally, no food or water for the first twenty-four hours. I told Steve what we had to do and we applied ourselves to these tasks.

Steve deployed the sea anchor, a device to slow the raft's movement through the water, while I made a start on the inventory. The large canvas bag was ideal for packing everything away in, to avoid having everything rolling chaotically around the bottom of the raft. I checked off the items in my mind as I placed them in the bag: 15½ litres of bottled water, two litres of bottled orange juice, one litre of long life milk, four 350 ml cans of lemonade, one 500 gram block of cheese, one 500 gram tin of salted peanuts, three apples, two 250 gram packets of glucose sweets, one 250 gram block of milk chocolate, one VHF hand-held radio, one packet of new flares which contained three rockets, two red hand-held and one orange smoke canister. There were six old rocket flares, four old red hand flares and four old smoke flares, and one torch and batteries. From two foil bags attached to the inside of the raft I added one set of raft instructions, one raft repair kit, one hand pump, one space blanket, two sponges, two red hand flares, one pack of seasickness tablets and two paddles.

In three small pockets in the raft I found one whistle, one safety knife, and one heaving line and quoit which I left in place. I packed everything neatly away in the canvas bag, making sure the flares and radio were easily accessible on the top, and zipped it shut. I left out the repair kit, sponges, pump and paddles. I opened the pack of seasickness tablets and took one and gave another to Steve.

Now that everything was packed away and everything was in its place, we could inspect the raft. Looking around it just didn't feel right. The canopy wasn't rigid and we seemed to be low in the water. It didn't take long to discover the problem; the top ring of the raft had failed to inflate. We both searched for damage and after a few minutes found the cause. The inflation valve of the top ring had blown out, leaving an open hole. Fuck this ancient life raft! That should just not happen. I searched in the small repair kit and found a couple of rubber bungs that looked like they were made for the job! I screwed and pushed one of the bungs into the opening, closing my eyes and straining with all my strength to push it in as hard as I could. Steve had the pump out and connected it to the valve. We took it in turns to pump up the top ring. Beautiful; it was nice and tight, the bung was holding. That looked and felt a lot better and it seemed to have doubled the interior space inside the raft. The canopy was rigid and the opening flaps could now be tightly secured.

Next I felt the bottom ring and decided that that could do with a bit of a top-up as well. We pumped some air into that until I was satisfied with the feel. The raft was fitted with a double bottom; in this case it was a separate inflatable mattress connected by webbing to the four corners of the raft. It resembled a square of bubble wrap, that stuff that kids love to pop in their fingers; only it was on a larger scale. Double bottoms are a good safety feature as they provide a layer of insulation between the occupants of the raft and the sea. Steve found the valve and soon had the double bottom inflated.

Next we sponged out the bottom of the raft until it was good and dry. I looked around and noticed a hole in the roof with what looked like a bag and a drawstring attached – the lookout position. Good, we could just stick our noggins through there and we would be able to scan the horizon for 360 degrees. I was able to safely secure the flaps and we both sat back, our little cocoon bucking wildly. But before I did this I had taken a long look around. There was nothing but the heaving sea. Night was setting in fast and I needed to think. "Okay, let's get comfortable," I said to Steve.

We settled ourselves, sitting with our backs against the side of the raft, and placed the canvas bag between us so it acted as an armrest. I opened the foil-backed space blanket. It was quite large and we wrapped ourselves up together. I could feel some body warmth being generated immediately and idly thought to myself, great things these space blankets. My head was spinning; everything had happened too fast. I needed to calm myself and take stock of the situation.

I began to think. We could be no further than eighty to ninety miles from Hong Kong. I had sent a mayday call on an international distress frequency and we had flares and a radio. I knew the shipping concentration was heavy in this area so the chances of being rescued were good. On top of all of this we had our supplies. With careful rationing, I thought we could make it last for ten days at least, if not fifteen. I explained all of this to Steve and he agreed. My last comment to him before settling down for the long night ahead was that all we had to do was sit tight, keep watch, conserve our energy and wait patiently to be rescued. At that point we had been on the raft for no longer than one hour but I was feeling exhausted. I lay my head on the bag between us, comforted by its contents, and closed my eyes.

I wanted to sleep but what happened next was the most terrifying moment of my life. There was no warning or time to prepare for it. With the thundering roar of a passing freight train, a breaking wave pitch poled the raft down its face. Over and over we went, arms and legs kicking and clawing, the water engulfing us. We were in a roaring, spinning ball of water. My mind raced in terror – so this is how I am going to die, this is how all shipwrecked sailors die. Oh God no!

The roar eventually subsided. I pushed my way up, gasping, and found a pocket of air in the upturned raft. I could hear Steve calling in the darkness. "You okay? You okay little buddy?"

"Yeah man, I'm okay."

We were in a bit of shock to say the least and we blindly kicked out and tore open the canopy. All we wanted to do was get out. "I'll go first," said Steve, as he duck dived and disappeared. A few seconds later he called out, "I'm okay, you can come out now." I held my breath, slid under the water and wriggled out of the opening in the canopy. I joined Steve clinging to the bottom of the capsized raft. It was pitch black, the wind was howling and the air was filled with the roar of the breaking waves. I was about to say something to Steve when I stopped in horror. The bag . . . *the bag*! Where was our bag with all our precious supplies and equipment? It would have been too heavy to float. Using our legs and feet we probed the upside down canopy. Nothing! It didn't take long to figure out what had happened. The canopy had acted like a funnel and the bag had just slid down the sides and dropped out of the opening.

I looked at Steve holding on to the other side of the raft, hair plastered against his head, and said to him, "We're in real trouble now mate – we're in big trouble."

We had to right the raft and get back inside it. My Maritime College training took over. We swam the raft around so it was facing the wind. Steve clambered up and took hold of the righting ropes on the far side of the raft and standing on the gas bottle at the entry he leaned back. I helped as much as I could and slowly, slowly, the raft lifted, until the wind caught it and it came crashing down on top of us as we pulled it upright. We swam out from underneath; it was textbook stuff. We heaved and pulled each other back into the raft, which was holding at least six inches of water. We searched desperately for anything that may have survived the capsizing; the bag was definitely history and all we found were two sponges and one paddle. It was obvious what we had to do next. I said to Steve, "We've got to get the water out of the raft."

We started, handful after handful, using the sponges to soak up the water. It was like emptying a bath full of water with just two sponges. An hour or so later, when we were down to the last few drops, I noticed the canopy flapping and buckling in the wind. In my confusion I hadn't realised that the top ring of the life raft had deflated. The capsizing must have blown the emergency rubber bung out of its hole. I just sat down and tried to take it all in. No food, no water, no flares, no radio, no repair kit, no pump – no nothing. All we had was half a raft, two sponges, a paddle, a safety knife, a coil of rope with a quoit and a whistle. Even the space blanket had disappeared. What a disaster. What a mother-fucking disaster, was all I could say to myself. But I said to Steve, "There's plenty of shipping in the area. We'll be spotted by one of them for sure tomorrow, so let's just get through the night."

We were saturated and would stay that way for the next eleven days. We were tired and confused, and no doubt in shock. Making ourselves as comfortable as we could, we tried to rest, but sleep was impossible. My mind was in turmoil, having been stripped bare of all the familiar comforts and necessities of life and thrown into the hungry sea. The voice of the stern lecturer at the Australian Maritime College passed through my mind: "Okay, gentlemen. You can live for three days without water and live without food for about seven. That's nature, and after that you are dead. And that's if hypothermia doesn't take you first." Shit! Three days! I don't want to die in three days time! Fuck! No way man, I was going to live longer than three days. This was the first target that I set myself.

My mind was dealing with these thoughts and a confused jumble of others when it happened again, the same as before, without warning. With a thunderous roar we were catapulted down the face of another breaking wave, over and over we went. Surely this must be it, raced through my mind as I cartwheeled under the crush of rubber and water. Gasping for air I found the air pocket and heard again, "You okay? You okay little buddy?"

"I'm okay. I'm okay," I repeated, coughing and choking up seawater.

"I'll go first," said Steve, for the second time that night, and disappeared under the water. A few seconds later he called out, "Okay. Your turn!" A deep breath and under I went again, emerging on the outside of the raft. Terror engulfed me as we clung to the upturned life raft in the middle of the ocean with the storm raging all around, all alone in the middle of the night. But we went straight again into the procedure of righting the raft and clambered back inside, collapsing into another six inches of water, as before.

"Let's get this water out," I said to Steve.

We groped for the sponges and found them floating around on top of the water. Without a word, one for one, we bailed the raft dry. Hours later, exhausted, we slumped back against the side of the raft. Shit, how much of this can I handle, I wearily asked myself. The night clearly wasn't anywhere near close to being over.

Twice more we capsized, each time as terrifying and shocking as before. On the last occasion we were so exhausted when we clambered onto the bottom of the capsized raft that we could do nothing more than just lie there. Maybe we could just lie here until the day comes, I thought to myself. The wind was howling and we were drenched from the capsizing and spray. Within minutes I was shivering uncontrollably and an alarm bell went off in my head. Get up, get up, get up, it urged. I had read many documents on survival at sea, particularly on life rafts that have been found floating upside down with the occupants dead from hypothermia, lying on top of their capsized rafts. I urged Steve, "Come on big fella, let's get this raft back up the right way and get the water out so we can get a bit of sleep. We're going to die if we stay up here."

We pulled ourselves together and were soon back inside the raft, the right way up. Kneeling in water up to our thighs, still drenched but a lot warmer, the canopy offered us some protection from the deadly wind chill factor and the certain death from hypothermia that would result from that. As I started bailing I told myself 'never lie on the top of a capsized raft again, you stupid old fool'.

After we made the raft dry yet again, we collapsed, wet and exhausted, where we knelt. A sullen grey and overcast dawn was spreading over the sky. I was totally exhausted and curled up into a ball and closed my eyes. We both slept through the day, stirring occasionally as a wave bounced and whipped us around. I had no dreams or thoughts; I was in no-man's-land. But eventually I slowly came to my senses. I uncurled my body, undid the opening flaps of the canopy and looked outside. It was beginning to get dark. A whole day had passed since the boat had sunk.

Day 2
Ships in the Night

I curled back up, desperately trying to get my brain around the events of the past forty-eight hours. It seemed a lifetime ago since I was in Hong Kong. Florida, Malan and Eddy would all be going about their daily business totally unaware of our plight, with Florida anxiously waiting for a call in the next day or so. I thought of our bag and the lost food, water, flares, torch and radio. I still could just not believe we had lost it and that everything we had was gone. We had absolutely no signalling device of any means, not even a match. We would have to be spotted to be rescued, and that meant that we had to make it through the night to have any chance of rescue the next day. It was as simple as that. We were wet, cold and shivering and I said to Steve, "Maybe we should lie together and see if we can get a bit warmer."

"Good idea mate. I'm freezing."

Before lying down we decided to sponge out the water, which had sprayed into the raft during the day. We got it nice and dry, even reaching under the double-bottomed mattress to remove the ever-present pool of water that had gathered there. We then lay down next to one another across the raft. That was better; the heat generated by our bodies soon helped us feel warmer. With the storm pushing us relentlessly onwards we entered the second night. And then it happened again. With the same thunderous roar we were pitched over and over by the massive force of a breaking sea. The same raw fear coursed through me, the same terrified thoughts. This time I am going to die! This time I am going to drown. But again I came up fighting for air in the black interior of the upturned raft. As usual Steve called out, "Are you okay little buddy?" and I replied, "Yes I'm okay but fuck me, man, this is bullshit! Really bullshit!"

"You're not wrong there," Steve replied.

We had the routine down pat by now; Steve swam out first and I followed. Steve then stood on the raft with the righting line, with me in the water helping keep the raft in position in the sea. A struggle, then up and over, pushing and pulling, and we were back inside the raft. But damn, there was water up to our waists as we sat there, still shaking from the shock of another sudden capsize. But there was no point in just sitting there; we had a job to do.

We found the sponges and started emptying out the water. It was a job that we couldn't just half do. We had to keep going until it was dry, pressing our sponges into all the holes in the bubble wrapped double bottom until every last drop was out, then reaching underneath to empty as much water as we could. We worked in a slow steady rhythm and after what seemed an age it was done. We closed the flaps and returned to our positions and cuddled up close, our clothes and bodies saturated. We didn't have much on; Steve was wearing a pair of jeans, a singlet and a woollen vest with a vinyl covering. I was wearing a pair of jeans and my woollen sea jumper. We hadn't had enough time or the opportunity to collect more clothing. So we had no socks, no woollen beanies, and no long johns. Nothing. We lay together and tried to sleep.

At some time during the night, through a fog in my brain, I heard something over the sound of the storm. I pulled myself awake and listened more closely. It was the drone of an approaching aircraft. I lurched up and struggled and fumbled to untie the flaps of the canopy. With a powerful throb of multiple engines a plane roared overhead – right smack overhead and at low level. I looked out but couldn't see a thing in the pitch-black night. The sound of the plane receded steadily downwind until I could hear nothing but the crashing of the sea again. I slumped back in the raft. "Fuck me, that thing passed straight fucking overhead!" I said to Steve.

I know a bit about planes; I have a library at home filled with books about boats and planes. This had been a multi-engine (possibly four), turbo-prop flying at low level. It had to have been a long-range maritime reconnaissance aircraft, exactly the type used in search and rescue missions. There was no other reason it would have been flying that low.

It was flying directly down our path so somebody must have heard my mayday. My heart was thumping. Maybe somebody knew where we were.

But my mood quickly turned to despair. We didn't have a single flare to alert them with; not even a torch. And it would have been so simple to have called them on the VHF radio. The distress frequency would have been monitored and they would have replied immediately. We would have been saved there and then. But with no sighting or signal, the plane would move on to the next leg of the search pattern and possibly never return. Why did it have to pass over at night? It would have spotted us during daylight. I couldn't stop cursing our bad luck.

We talked for a while about the plane, trying to find a positive side. Perhaps its appearance meant that someone had heard my mayday call? I assured Steve that during the day we would definitely be seen and rescued, and we returned to our sleeping positions and our own thoughts. I slipped into a fitful sleep, berating myself as I drifted off. Why hadn't I secured the bag to the raft? Shit, how could I have been that stupid? Why hadn't I thought of that? Fuck me, we lost everything; how could I have possibly been that dumb? We might have been saved right now! The plane would have seen our flare and be circling, having alerted a ship. I tried to sleep but I felt frustrated, guilty and angry.

An hour or so later – I couldn't tell how long I'd slept – I was woken by another roar. I took a deep breath as the avalanche of monsters crashed down on us. Water, arms and legs; confusion as the wave swept on by.

An hour later we were still sponging out the last of the water, having uprighted the raft yet again. Leaning through the canopy flaps to wring water out of my sponge, I spotted a light disappearing behind a rushing wave. "There's a light!" I shouted excitedly. We strained our eyes into the night. "There! There it is again!" I pointed in the direction of the sighting, nearly directly upwind of us. A few minutes later I had it; it was a ship. I could see two white lights and one red. "It's a freighter and it'll pass close on our port side," I said to Steve. We watched the lights approaching. Sure enough it was a large freighter.

"Shit!" I said for the hundredth time. One miserable flare and we would soon be sitting all wrapped up in the galley of the freighter, drinking hot coffee. I banged my fist in frustration on the side of the raft and we could only watch as the ship passed by us about half a mile on our port side. Its masthead and red sidelight slowly faded, and were replaced by a single white stern light. I strained my neck around the side of the raft canopy to watch it fade away into the night.

"Shit, there's another one!" I shouted. This one was going to be closer, much closer. The white masthead lights were nearly on top of each other, but a red light was still visible. She was coming upwind and we were in danger of her running us down. I could hear the steady thump, thump, thump, thump of her propellers thrashing the water. This was going to be close. I shuddered at the thought of being run down by the ship, dragged under the bows and chewed up by the propellers. I could see her clearly now, high out of the water as she passed by close on her port side, her propellers breaking the surface. I could see tiny figures high in the wheelhouse; I could have shone a torch in their faces – if I'd had one. But we were in total darkness as she passed not more than one hundred metres away.

I blew the whistle non-stop and Steve shouted at the top of his voice but it was, of course, useless; our pitiful sounds carrying away in the wind like puffs of smoke. The freighter disappeared as quickly as she had appeared, leaving us staring, dumbstruck, into the blackness. I couldn't believe it, a plane and then two ships! We could have been saved! They were so strong and safe, and so close. Again I was tormented by the loss of the bag. One miserable flare, even a torch and we would have been saved. We'd have been safe and secure. But there was nothing to do but close the flaps and lie back down.

I thought of the plane and the two ships. Was it a coincidence that all of these were heading pretty much directly along our track? They must be looking for us, I thought. Curse the *night*! Curse our *bad luck*! But with a search underway, we would be rescued when day came, definitely.

Swampings became more frequent. Breaking waves slammed against the canopy, sending torrents of cold seawater pouring into the raft. Every time this happened we would get back on our knees without a word and sponge the water out. We struggled throughout the night, suffering one more chaotic capsizing and numerous swampings. We did what we had to do as a matter of survival. If we didn't bail and dry the raft we would die from hypothermia. And neither of us wanted to die. It was freezing cold and we cuddled together, waiting and praying for the morning to arrive. The only physical comfort I had experienced since being on the raft had been when I pissed for the first time, luxuriating in the warmth of the urine running down my legs and thighs.

The dawn eventually crept over us. The sun wasn't visible but we could sense its presence as the temperature rose a few critical degrees. "Today we will be saved mate," I said to Steve. "There is plenty of shipping around."

For the first time my thoughts returned to our boat. What the hell had happened? What catastrophic event had taken place in the engine room? Words and comments flew around my brain – "You guys are crazy", "that boat", "that boat", "You are very brave". I searched for an explanation, for some reason why we were battling for our lives in a life raft, but I found none. I thought of every thing I had lost – all of my possessions, all of my treasures that I had carried with me from command to command. The framed photograph of my beautiful children, Sophie and Daniel, and another of my mother and father, always hung where I could see them from my bunk. My current and old passport and sea service record. I had long dreamed of writing a book of my many adventures exploring the world as a fisherman. These documents were going to be my references; they clearly and precisely charted my life's course. Dates, times, places, vessel names, all with a stamp of officialdom. New Caledonia, Fiji, Western Samoa, Tonga, Port Moresby, Lae, Calcutta, Madras, Andaman Islands, Penang, Singapore, Cape Town, Namibia, Tokyo, Osaka, New Zealand and more. Not to mention every major fishing port on the coastline of Australia. Every name and place had a story to tell. They were gone forever, along with my wallet. The money, credit cards and licences could all be replaced, but Florida . . . her contact address and telephone number, my only links to her, lay carefully folded in my wallet, on the dark ocean floor.

I was in despair. Florida would still be going about her life and waiting happily for my call, unaware of my deadly struggle. As I lay cuddled up next to Steve, silent tears ran down my face. I knew that whatever happened, I would never see Florida again. We were like ships in the night.

My life was becoming a living nightmare, with both the physical and mental torture growing in intensity. I had to remain convinced that we would be saved. One of the cardinal rules of being stranded in a life raft was to always keep a look out, which makes a lot of sense, so that we would spot potential rescuers and alert them to our presence. But this hardly applied to us, as we had absolutely no means of alerting anyone; all we could do was to spot them. A crucial factor for us was that we had to be seen by another human being to be rescued, or make it to land on our own. I felt a bit guilty for not keeping watch, but it was a serious waste of time and energy. During the frequent bailouts we scanned the horizon continually, but there was nothing to be seen except the dark green of the towering sea and the grey of the low hanging clouds.

It was during one of these bailing sessions that I noticed a group of fish swimming along with us. Sometimes they swam under the raft, sometimes they trailed along a few feet behind. "Look Steve, fish!" I said. We peered down and looked at the fish, both of us having the same thought; how to catch one? I pictured myself sitting back, enjoying a serve of sashimi. Just fantastic, I thought.

The appearance of the fish was not surprising to me. The raft was acting like an FAD, or fish aggregation device, used throughout the world as a means to attract and catch fish. In nature, these were logs of wood or floating masses of seaweed. Man-made ones were any simple raft or structure that could be anchored to the seabed. Small fish would seek shelter near the FAD and this, in turn, would attract larger predators. They were very successful in attracting fish.

The fish were tantalisingly close. Steve made a few quick grabs, but they easily avoided his plunging hands. We finished drying the raft out and sat back to see if we could come up with some way to catch a fish. For the first time since getting onto the raft we had something positive to do, something to occupy our minds.

We went through our possessions – a blunt-ended safety knife with a two-inch blade, a paddle, a plastic whistle, a piece of rope, two sponges and a piece of plastic I had found under the double bottom. I didn't know what it was or its purpose. It resembled a tiny witch's hat, open at the ends and complete with a wide brim. It was pretty easy to figure out what to do. Steve set about the task of lashing the knife to the handle of the paddle and made a rudimentary spear. I sat studying the whistle and witch's hat, to see if there was any way I could fashion a hook. I rejected the whistle, basically an oblong shape of hard plastic, and concentrated on the witch's hat. If I cut the top off the hat it would leave a circular brim or washer. Over this washer shape I mentally drew the shape of a hook. Yes, given a bit of time I should be able to fashion a hook of sorts, but I would need the knife. As the spear was our best bet to start with, I stuffed the little hat into my jeans and helped Steve with the job of tightly lashing the knife to the paddle. We tied our length of rope to the other end and it was done. A spear with a safety line attached. We could not afford to lose the knife or the paddle.

We took it in turns, lying with our bodies stretched over the side of the raft, arm outstretched, waiting to strike when a fish came within range, but we didn't even get close. The fish were far too quick, darting away as soon as our spear hit the water. All afternoon we persevered, but in the end we had to concede that the fish had wised up, swimming well out of range of our puny missile. "Not to worry, tomorrow I will make a hook and we will have a go with that," I told Steve.

As the darkness started to creep across the sky, our third night on the raft was about to begin.

Day 3
Setting the Target

I was beginning to hate and fear the nights. We were a minute, invisible dot in the vastness of the heaving sea. Any chance of rescue faded to nothing as the blackness descended and all of our capsizing happened at night, as the wind tended to strengthen at nightfall and then gradually ease as dawn broke. So we had nothing but these to look forward to and to survive, with hours on our knees bailing out the water each time we were flipped over.

I tried to prepare myself for this ordeal, but for the very first time I began to think about water and food. Would I die of thirst today? No way! No way was I going to die today, I told myself. For the last two days we had just been surviving, battling to right the raft and clear the water from it. We were saturated, cold and exhausted, cuddled up together on the double-bottomed mattress. My mind was in turmoil as I searched for reasons, for answers to why I was here. I kept telling myself that there was no way I was going to die today. And besides, I didn't feel too bad – physically, that is. I wasn't really hungry and I wasn't really thirsty, just cold, wet, and totally miserable. I lifted my jumper and looked at my tummy. It was still its usual shape, with the small bulge of extra flesh extending from my rib cage to my navel. I called it ageing – it was nothing at all to do with the few beers I had consumed during the twenty years I had spent as a fisherman. But the rough life had also demanded a certain level of fitness and I was in pretty reasonable shape. I patted my belly. I am going to need you in the next few days, I said to myself. Before I pulled my jumper back down I noticed one or two small red dots on my pale skin.

Without warning we were hit by another breaking sea. This time we did not capsize but were badly swamped, the raft spinning like a top, its canopy collapsing and flapping wildly against our bodies. It's started, I groaned to myself. We had learnt very early on that the raft could only face in one direction, with the canopy opening facing us into the wind and the sea. The other way around and the canopy would collapse. Whether this was due to the design of the raft, or the deflated upper buoyancy ring, we didn't know. But we had a routine worked out for this event. I would lie on my back and grasp the canopy and pull it down to my chest to stop its wild flogging and Steve would paddle us around until we were facing in the right direction again. As soon as we rounded into the sea the canopy would snap back tight again.

I found myself lying up to my chest in water with barely any freeboard, the water slopping out of the raft as we were buffeted by the storm. "Fuck we got a gutfull that time!" I got to my knees to start the long process of bailing out the water.

"Where is my sponge, see my sponge anywhere?" I asked Steve.

"Can't see it this side," he said, after a look around.

We groped frantically under the double bottom but it was gone; it must have floated out with the water gushing out after the last swamping. Shit! How could I have been that careless, one of our precious sponges, the only thing, it seemed to me, that had stood between death and us. I cursed into the wind. Steve looked down at his sponge, tore it in half and handed me one of the pieces. "Let's get on with it," he said.

It was now going to take us twice the time to empty the raft. There was only one way I could cope, and that was by going into a semi-trance as I started to mop up. I came to call it my mantra: one handful for Sophie, one handful for Daniel, one for Sophie, one for Daniel, Sophie, Daniel, Sophie, Daniel. I repeated it a thousand times as I rocked back and forth with the sponge full of water. An age later I finished my silent chant and the raft was empty and we could lie down.

During the search for the sponge I had dragged out the two plastic bags that had contained the raft's equipment. They had been lying under the double bottom still attached to the raft by a small length of rope. On closer inspection,

I realised that these bags were not plastic at all but were made of the same material as the space blankets. I offered one of the soggy bags to Steve, who eyed it with disdain. "I'm alright mate, you can have them," he said.

I slipped my feet into one of the bags and they fitted in snugly. I split the other bag down one of its sides and I had a hood. I pulled the neck of my jumper up as far as I could, stretching it past my ears and nose. When I lay down this would hold my new hood firmly to my head. With a bit more pulling and stretching, I managed to cover my hands by clenching the sleeve ends tightly in my fists. I lay down and cuddled up next to Steve. It was heaps better; I could feel some warmth in my head and feet. I had covered all my extremities where heat loss is the greatest, because heat means energy and I needed all my energy if I was going to live. The next thing was to relax and conserve what reserves I had left. I lay there telling myself that I would get through that night, and then there would be a whole new day when we might be saved. Tomorrow we would be saved.

I closed my eyes and listened to the roar of the sea breaking all around us. I counted the seconds between each successive roar, trying to gauge the storm. Was it intensifying or was it slackening? It gave me something to think about, away from unthinkable thoughts that had started to creep into my head. We drifted on before the wind, lying across the raft like two people in a lovers' embrace, our feet, legs and arms closely entwined. There was no embarrassment or timidity; it was a necessity to protect us from the elements. The person on the inner of our spoon position was the most comfortable. His back was covered, as he lay curled up with his hands between his legs. He was also the most exposed and any water bursting through the canopy opening would hit him fair in the chest. As he was the closest, it was his responsibility to refasten the Velcro fastenings that held the flaps closed when the in-rushing sea or wind tore them apart. There was no best position and we swapped regularly during the long night to ensure that our work effort remained equal.

There was no escape from the terror of the night as we capsized twice. Twice we had to right the raft and kneel side by side in the darkness sponging out the water, in silence, me with my mantra of Sophie, Daniel, Sophie, Daniel, beating a rhythm in my head, Steve with his own private thoughts. For every action we had a reaction; we either bailed out the water or we died. There was no complaining, there were no arguments; we did what we had to do, as often as we had to do it, until the job was finished.

During the short respite between the capsizes that night, Steve stirred and said to me, his voice exhausted, "I hate the nights."

"Same here, I hate the nights."

We were going to repeat those words often in the forthcoming days.

At last, a tiny bit of warmth crept across my back and dawn arrived. We had survived another night and I assured myself that today we would be saved. I lay there counting off the roar of each wave. Their frequency had definitely slowed; the wind had again eased at dawn. Thoughts of my children, family and friends passed through my head. We were only just due to arrive in the Philippines, so no one would be concerned yet. Nobody would have any idea that we were missing, lost at sea. It was too much to comprehend. I pushed the thoughts back deep into my mind and tried to think positively. Today we will be rescued. Today I would make a hook. Today it would surely rain. I checked myself over mentally and I was okay, I didn't feel like I was dying. I made a promise to myself – that today I would live. There was no way I was going to die that day.

Steve stirred and together we unwound ourselves from our embrace and stretched, grimacing as our cramped legs and arms came to life. I rested up against the side of the raft. "Okay, Steve, let's unlash that knife. I'm going to try to make a hook. Fish for dinner!"

I found the little plastic hat in my pocket and was examining it when Steve handed me the knife. The first job was to cut the end or top off the hat to finish up with the washer shape that I was looking for. I pushed the knife across the plastic and it made hardly a scratch. Shit, this was going to take all day. I pushed harder and could see a tiny groove this time. Oh well, I had nothing better to do so I absorbed myself in the task. A good hour later I had managed to hack away the top section of the hat shape, leaving me with a flat plastic washer in my hand. I then started chipping away at the ring, shaping the hook as I went. Tiny pieces of red plastic fell down on my jumper. The knife was totally blunt on the end so as not to puncture the raft and it was getting blunter and blunter. I persevered for another couple of hours.

Finally, with badly cramped fingers I became the proud owner of a plastic hook, complete with barb and eye. We had no bait so I decided on a lure. I untwisted some of our heaving line and teased out the fibres, which I lashed to the eye of the hook. Then I attached the hook to the heaving line. I threw it over the side, where our friendly fish were still in perfect formation. And then we waited.

I had pretty much decided before I started that this would be a dubious undertaking, and as the plastic hook and line floated uselessly on the surface, I became convinced that it was going to be one hell of a stupid fish to get itself caught on that. The fish didn't even give it a second look. "Oh well, at least we tried," I said to Steve, with a rueful smile.

While I was idly picking the red pieces of plastic off my jumper and throwing them into the sea, I noticed two things. First, that we had lost our sea anchor; the retaining ring had torn off the raft. It must have happened overnight in one of the wild capsizes. It certainly hadn't helped to keep us upright, that's for sure, so it was no great loss. But I also noticed that the bits of red plastic I was throwing into the sea were disappearing quickly behind us, trailing steadily away from the raft. I looked closely at the fish; they were not swimming aimlessly around but were steadily swimming in a tiny school, purposefully working as they kept pace with the raft.

I put my hand and arm into the sea and could feel the movement of the water flowing past. We had to be doing two knots, maybe more. We were moving, and we were making distance. A plan began to form in my mind but

I needed to make some calculations and think about it. First I needed to estimate our speed, as this was the crucial part of this exercise. Mental arithmetic comes naturally to me; it's part of a captain's life, constantly doing sums. How far, how long, how much fuel, courses, bearings, speed, navigating, timing and more. I measured the heaving line between my arms, and it was a bit over twenty metres. I then tied a knot to the end of it and measured back twenty metres and tied another knot, leaving a few more metres up to the rubber quoit. While Steve operated the line, I closed my eyes and counted. He let the quoit into the water and paid it out, stopping at the first knot. Waiting until the coil had grabbed the sea and was pulling tight on the line, he said, "Go!" and let the line pay out. I counted: one thousand, two thousand, three thousand, four . . . When Steve said, "Stop" I was up to eighteen thousand. So this was eighteen seconds for twenty metres.

"Okay, let's do this a few times more," I said. We repeated the exercise ten times, Steve paying out the line and me counting – eighteen, sixteen, eighteen, fifteen, seventeen. A pattern was emerging. I settled on an average of seventeen seconds and sat back to do some maths; seventeen seconds for twenty metres. I calculated that that was roughly seventy metres a minute. Okay then, seventy times sixty is four thousand, two hundred metres in one hour. Now very roughly again, one nautical mile is the equivalent of two kilometres. I had it – we were doing approximately 2.1 knots through the water. So far so good.

Steve was following all of this with interest. I told him that next I had to figure the current. "Let's look at the sea for a while and see what we think." We had been looking at the sea for nearly three days now and were getting used to its appearance. It was still blowing a steady thirty knots; there was no real swell, just a four to five metre breaking sea; breaking, not curling, the wave period not too tight. I had spent years watching the sea and comparing the movements on my computer screens and plotters. And I know currents; it is part of my job. I had searched for the large pelagic species on the edges of these great machines, the driving force of the oceans which give them life. Some days you can almost see the flow, a different shimmering on the surface of the water; different from the patterns caused by the wind and the waves.

I knew that our direction of travel was roughly west-south-west, following the landmass of southern China. In general, currents run along the continental shelves following the lie of the land; in other words, the current flow was either directly behind us or directly in front of us. Coming from the sides would not be an option. After some further deliberations, I said to Steve, "I reckon the current is right up our arse, I bet my bottom dollar on it," and he agreed.

I remembered my space blanket bags had little tin grommets on their corners for the retaining rope that attached them to the raft. Using the knife I prised them off and carefully tossed them into the sea just in front of the raft and off to the side. I watched them sink. Sure enough, they were angling down in the direction of our travel. That settled it and we needed some good news. The raft was blowing downwind and was being assisted in its passage by a favourable current; we could be doing two and a half to three knots. I had no way of gauging the speed of the current, but from experience I added half a knot to my speed-over-the-water calculation. We were covering at least sixty nautical miles a day. Even now after three days, we were close to two hundred nautical miles from our sinking position.

I closed my eyes and pictured the large-scale chart of the South China Sea, the chart I had been using after I cleared Hong Kong. The coastline of China ran pretty much east west. Somewhere to the west lay the large Chinese island of Hainan and well to the south of Hainan Island were the Paracels, a lonely uninhabited group of low-lying coral atolls. Through this gap and further on lay Vietnam.

Night was approaching and I looked at the sky, trying to estimate the position of the setting sun through the thick clouds. I was positive that it was setting more behind us rather than to our side. This tallied with what I had been thinking before we sank; the wind had been coming from the east and I estimated our course as west-south-west.

Now for the distances. Again I closed my eyes and recollected the chart. My globe and a large world map had pride of place in the lounge room of the house I shared with my young brother, Andrew, in Hobart in Tasmania. I put my imagery dividers on Hong Kong and then opened them out to the Philippines, a distance that I knew. I then swung them around to our course. The distance was further than that, maybe by another third, possibly even more, between our sinking position and Vietnam. I settled on eight hundred nautical miles. We had already covered one hundred and eighty or so, so that left six hundred and twenty. At about sixty nautical miles a day, it was going to take ten more days to reach Vietnam. "If we don't get picked up we have to survive for ten days, Steve. We'll come ashore in Vietnam."

I had achieved my first goal by surviving the past three days. I certainly didn't feel like I was dying, I was nowhere close to it. I set my next target; I was going to live for the next ten days, there was no way I was just going to die.

We secured the canopy carefully with the Velcro fastener, lay down together and waited for the approaching night. Ten days, ten days, I must live for ten days, I repeated to myself, as my exhausted body succumbed to sleep.

Day 4
The Oil Field

I was woken by a tremendous roar. Tensing my body in readiness for the impact, a split second of fear engulfed me as the wave slammed into us. Disorientated and spinning in the cold water, I fought to find the air pocket.

"You okay buddy?"

"I'm okay," I replied.

It took a few seconds to clear and cough water out of my mouth and throat before the adrenalin flowed again. "Let's get on with it, eh?" I said.

This was the bit I hated the most – holding my breath, sinking under the water to wriggle out of the canopy opening to come out the other side. I didn't like going under the water, I never had; it was an unnatural thing to do. If we were meant to be underwater, God would have given us gills. And I've always had an unspoken fear of drowning; for me, it would be the worst possible way to go. I can remember reading the account of the *Andrea Gail* in Sebastian Junger's 'The Perfect Storm'. When I got to the drowning part I had stopped abruptly, unable to read on, sweat pouring down my back; and I flipped over three or four pages before I continued reading. I just didn't want to know about it. A paradox, I know. I quite happily go to sea and yet my biggest fear is drowning.

We righted the raft and clambered inside, soaked and shaken. "Fuck! Where's my sponge? Steve! Do you see my sponge anywhere?" I searched frantically, groping under the double bottom. There it was. Relief washed over me and I whipped myself mentally. You stupid fucking idiot! Don't you ever let that sponge go again! We knelt together in the centre of the raft and started the long and torturous job of bailing out again. Sophie, Daniel, I chanted in my head, as the minutes turned to hours before the last few drops were squeezed out. I rolled up my sponge and pushed it into my jeans. "Sponge in pocket!" I said aloud, as I patted my pocket.

"Good idea mate," said Steve. He did the same thing and repeated, "Sponge in pocket."

As terrifying as they always were, the last being no easier to endure than the first, we were getting used to the capsizings. We were becoming raft veterans, and had got the routine down pat; we each knew our jobs right down to the check and call of "Sponge in pocket." The routine gave us some reassurance; it had become our main purpose in life – our only purpose. It gave some meaning to our daily existence, some order when we had lost control of everything else. We either followed this routine unquestionably or we died, and giving up was not an option for me. I had decided I was going to fight with every breath in my body. I would never give up – that would be like committing suicide, and I would never do it; the very thought repelled me.

I went through my personal routine to prepare myself for the night, carefully wrapping my body up with the help of my foil 'socks' and hood as carefully as I could, to maintain my body heat and strength. I then took up my position next to Steve and started counting breakers. I was keeping in tune to the sound of the crashing waves, picking out the ones that were breaking and passing just metres on either side of the raft from the dangerous ones, the ones that would swamp us or cause another capsize. The noise from the storm throughout our entire ordeal was deafening; it was like sitting in the middle of a ten-lane super highway with your eyes closed, with speeding semi-trailers roaring past. It felt like standing blindfolded in a torture chamber, terrified, not knowing when the next strike would fall. "Hate the nights," I said aloud.

"Hate the nights," replied Steve.

One, two or three hours later – I couldn't tell – we were cursing again, frustrated, cold, wet and exhausted, pushing ourselves to our knees and reaching into our pockets for our sponges. Routine – routine – routine . . . over and over and over – bailing out the raft. An age later we lay collapsed together again, muscles tensing every time a wave roared past, inches from the raft.

A short while after that, a small wave splashed in, pushing the canopy open. This shipped only a small amount of water but as it had already drained under the double bottom we decided it wasn't enough to cause any discomfort. Steve got up to re-secure the flapping opening and as he did so, checked around the horizon. "Ships mate! Ships!" he cried.

Lying in the foetal position, still half asleep, I struggled to clear my brain. Not moving, I said, "A ship in the night only brings frustration and despair."

"Right in front of us mate! Five, six, no seven! Fuck they're everywhere, right in front!" he cried excitedly.

I was up in a flash. There were six or seven ships dead ahead. What was going on? I stuck my head outside and pushed down the canopy to look in the direction of travel. "They're not ships mate, it's an oil field. They're oil rigs," I said.

We seemed to be heading straight at the closest rig, not even a mile away. A monster of human creation, solid steel towering over the storm and lit up like a Christmas tree; it stood on its four massive legs, a safe haven. In awe and anticipation, we knelt in the raft, holding down the canopy, watching its approach. "I think we're going to miss it, but not by much," I said to Steve. We were closing fast, and were by then about four hundred metres away.

"I'm swimming for it," said Steve, and immediately started to strip off his vest.

I was shocked. "What?" was all I could manage to say.

"I said I am going to swim for it. I don't care what you do."

I said "You can't, you'll never get there, you'll never make it in this sea and current. You'll kill yourself and you'll kill me! I can't manage the raft alone. You'll kill yourself and you'll kill me!" I shouted to him.

"I don't care, I'm swimming for it!" he retorted.

I pleaded with him. "How are you going to get up there?" I pointed to the platform now towering high above us. "There are no fucking neat little landing platforms and handy staircases on an oil rig. You'll get smashed to pieces and die! You can't do it Steve, you just can't do it."

He was taking off his jeans – fuck! He was really going to do it. This was madness. His next comment shocked me again, and cut deep. He said, "And when we get up there, I'm going to give you a bashing!"

"What? I asked, not comprehending.

"You heard me! I'm going to give you a bashing for nearly killing me!" he replied angrily.

I didn't need that. I was speechless. As I watched, dumbfounded, he prepared to dive out of the raft. I had to stop him. I had to, otherwise we were both dead. I tried again. "Don't do it Steve! You're going to drown yourself. All our effort, just like that, to end like this?" I pleaded.

We were a lot closer to the rig by then, about two hundred metres away. I reckoned we would pass no more than one hundred metres from it; we could see the rig clearly, the waves smashing into its massive legs sending spray and foam up thirty metres or more. We could see a spider web of thick mooring cables extending out into the sea from all corners of the rig, deadly scythes in the heaving sea. There were no landing platforms, no catwalks or stairways. I yelled to Steve through the howling wind as I pointed at the rig, "Look, look! You'll be smashed to pieces, cut to ribbons, even if you get there. Don't do it!"

Steve looked and hesitated. I watched him anxiously while the reality slowly took hold of him and his new found hope of being saved drained from his body, as the realisation reluctantly dawned on him that to swim for it was clearly suicide. He slumped back in the raft.

I grabbed the whistle and started blowing. We were already alongside the rig and passing fast. I could hear the machinery over the wind and could see a man wearing a blue hard hat on a catwalk high above; but he never looked in our direction. We were invisible in the darkness, the whistle undetectable over the sounds of the rig and the screaming wind and roaring sea. And then it was gone, dropping away behind us. I scanned the horizon and detected another six rigs, their waste gas flares lighting the night sky, and what looked like a tanker moored at its filling station. I could see one more rig deep on the horizon, a few tiny lights. I watched the one we had just passed grow smaller and smaller and closed the flaps.

Steve was in a corner of the raft, kneeling, bowed over, his hands covering his face. I curled up in the middle of the raft and tried to organise my mind. What did Steve mean, I had nearly killed him? *Was* I going to kill him, was I responsible for this nightmare? The questions raced and tumbled around my confused mind; I wasn't ready for this – how was I going to cope with this? I cursed the night again and again and every fucking chance of rescue that had passed us by in the middle of the night. I just could not believe our run of bad luck.

I lay shivering in a small pool of water. The mental torture had started and it was cold. I said quietly to Steve, who hadn't moved, "C'mon mate, we had better cuddle up, eh?"

"Yeah mate; yeah mate," he said back.

After we had organised ourselves and tucked up tight, Steve murmured, "Sorry about before mate."

"Don't worry about it, in one ear and out the other. I can't even remember what you said."

"Hate the nights."

"Hate the nights."

And we left it at that.

I slowly woke with the tepid warmth of the awakening day. Getting groggily to my knees, I opened the flaps and looked around. From horizon to horizon there was nothing but the heaving sea, not a rig in sight. We were alone again in the ocean.

I tried to think positively; we surely must be moving fast to clear the entire oil field in a few short hours. I dredged my memory for the chart of the South China Sea and could vaguely remember seeing an oil field marked. I hadn't paid it too much attention when I was studying the chart; I had been concentrating on my route from Hong Kong to the Philippines, but could remember seeing it far to the west of our planned track and on the edge of the continental shelf. So that was good news and bad news, I thought. The good news was that we were still high in latitude and the wind must be even more to the east than I had calculated. This meant that we were on course to miss Hainan Island and well clear of the more dangerous isolated and uninhabited Paracel Islands – and right on course to hit Vietnam square in the middle. The bad news, I thought to myself, was that we were out of the sea-lanes and our chances of being rescued by a passing ship had diminished to just about zero. It was getting clearer in my mind that to live, we had to make it to Vietnam – we had to live in this raft with nothing for ten days.

I started to think about food and water and my stomach growled and tightened. I was hungry and I was thirsty. I had read most of the survival epics and thought of the stories of cracked mouths or swollen tongues and parched throats. I ran my tongue around my lips; they weren't cracked, my tongue wasn't swollen and my throat wasn't parched. I was thirsty, but I didn't feel as though I was going to die of thirst today.

Steve was up, or rather, on his knees. We decided to sponge the remnants of the water from the night out of the raft –

we may as well be as comfortable as we could be – and we got the raft nice and dry. The wind had eased a fraction and I hoped that maybe we would get some respite from it for a few hours. There were only two positions we could get in, kneeling up or lying down, and I lay back down.

Steve suddenly piped up, "I'm going to drink my piss." I looked up and he was studying the plastic handle of the paddle. He unscrewed the handle and found what he was looking for, a cup, six inches deep and an inch in diameter, where the handle had been. "This will do," he said, and unzipped his jeans.

I looked on with interest. He raised the end of the paddle to his mouth, blocked his nose and swallowed. He gagged, fighting to keep it down. How gross, I thought to myself. I wasn't ready to drink my own, not yet anyway. He emptied his bladder with another three or four shots, all accompanied by dry retching. Fuck me! Is this what life's come to, drinking our own piss to stay alive? I thought back to Hong Kong and all the beautiful food and drinks we'd consumed, and where we were happy, with not a care in the world. It didn't seem real, it felt like a lifetime ago, another world. I blocked the thought from my mind because it didn't bear thinking about.

We slept for a while. The raft was dry and a slight warmth had penetrated the enclosed space. This was the most comfortable we had been since jumping on the raft nearly four days ago. I woke a few hours later and looked at the legs of my jeans. Shit hot! There were a couple of dry patches around the knees – another first! Our clothes had been totally soaked for four days. I knelt up and opened the canopy flaps and studied the empty ocean. The sea had definitely lost its sting and the wind was still blowing steadily, but maybe just under thirty knots now. The cloud cover had lifted and there was no sign of the rain I had expected. With my limited knowledge of the weather in this area, I had associated the monsoon with rain.

Our friends the fish were still swimming steadily as they kept in formation behind the raft. I put my hand in the water and felt its flow; we were still moving along at a good pace. As much as I hated the wind and the sea, the cause of all our discomfort and horror, the wind must not stop, we needed it to survive. If it stopped blowing we would literally be dead in the water – we would be sitting there nice and dry on a calm ocean, but would slowly die of thirst and hunger. I looked at the sky and murmured, "Blow, you bastard, blow." I closed the canopy, pressing as tightly as I could on the Velcro fastenings as I worked my way down. The raft was at last dry and warm enough to stretch out a bit. I rested my feet on the inflated ring and stretched out on my back, looking absently at the orange canopy tightening against the wind, and tried to order my thoughts.

I had the same jumbled list of questions: why was I here, was anybody looking for us, did anybody know we were missing, how long can we last, *have* I killed Steve, why did we lose the bag, why did I sail without an EPIRB? And if this wasn't bad enough, flying at tangents to these thoughts were even darker ones; my children, my darling children, my family and friends. Dear God, I thought, none of them would know what had happened to me. Sophie and Daniel would be happily and excitedly looking forward to seeing their daddy at Christmas time. My mind worked overtime. There were no answers, no comfort, we were lost, alone and fighting for our lives; no one was going to help us. I vowed to myself that I would not let my children down. I would not give up hope of rescue. It could happen any time – in ten minutes or tomorrow morning. In the meantime I had to live. Worrying uses energy, I told myself, I must conserve my energy. I pulled the neck of my sodden jumper up over my ears, closed my eyes and forced the despair from my mind. I thought of food as the raft pushed and heaved its way through the ocean in the fading light.

Day 5
Eat Me if I Die

"Hate the nights," I mumbled to myself after yet another capsizing.

It was starting to get cold and the wind was picking up again. We sponged out the raft and made ourselves as comfortable as we could. There was no rush, we weren't going anywhere. I took my time to make sure I was covered up as well as I possibly could be, determined to save every ounce of energy that I could. Once my preparations were completed I eased myself into position next to Steve and cuddled up as tight as I could. Hate the nights, I repeated to myself. There was no hope of rescue; we were freezing cold and we were wet, exhausted, thirsty and hungry. I set myself a new target: I had to survive the night to have a chance of rescue the next day – survive the night, just survive the night, I said to myself as I closed my eyes and tried to sleep.

I thought of my heroes, dead or alive, who had shaped my life from an early age: Mathew Flinders, Captain Cook, Ernst Shackleton, Francis Chichester, Captain Bligh, Hillary and Tenzing, Scott of the Antarctic, Chuck Yeager, Horatio Nelson and others of the same ilk. They all had one thing in common – they all had a steadfast determination to succeed and survive under the most horrific and arduous of conditions. I had read and re-read their adventures with awe and respect; I could remember wondering how they had managed to survive. Did they have special powers; were they one of a kind? I had taken the view a long time ago that mankind in general was getting weaker. We have comfortable houses, cars, planes, offices, mobile phones and sedentary jobs which bring the money rolling in to purchase more and more luxuries. There is no reason to do it tough any more and people in general have lost the skills, the genes of raw survival. I often wondered how I would have coped, climbing a yardarm in a gale, punching in the canvas to secure the sails dressed only in rudimentary oilskins, my fingernails torn and my feet bare; the only respite being to go off watch to a wet and cold bunk and eat weevil-infected hard tack and drink sour water. My answer was always the same; I couldn't possibly have done it, and no one could these days.

But I had begun to think differently. I was fighting for my life and I was determined to take a page from my heroes' books and be like them – I was going to beat the odds, I was never going to give up. I was going to survive and succeed, and with these thoughts I drifted off to sleep. I was busy trudging through blinding snow, my face covered in ice, dragging an overloaded sled, when a deafening roar filled my ears. "An avalanche! An avalanche!" I cried out in my sleep.

The breaking wave hit us hard and instantly the terror of my nightmare became a reality. Over and over we went, terrified and fighting for air. Coughing and spluttering I regained my senses as I forced my head up into the small air pocket, taking deep breaths as I calmed myself down. Exiting the raft, I clung to the overturned rubber, my despair as overwhelming as always. I was wondering how much more I could take, when a large wave pushed roughly under us and I lost my grip on the raft and found myself floundering in the water, with nothing to hold on to.

"Little buddy, little buddy, *swim!*" I heard Steve screaming. I struck out blindly in the direction of his voice. "*Swim! Swim, man!*" Steve was calling.

My stretched woollen jumper and jeans felt like lead weights. Don't panic, don't panic – just swim, fired through my head. I kicked my way harder through the water and was reaching my limits when I felt Steve's hand grasp my thrashing arm. "You're okay now, you're okay now," Steve reassured me, as I clung to the upturned raft like a limpet.

Fuck me, that was real scary. I thought I was gone then, I thought I was fucked. My heart was pounding – my worst nightmare, my greatest fear, was to be left alone in the ocean to drown. I tried to pull myself together, to regain some strength; we had to get this raft back up and emptied. By the time the whole routine of uprighting and bailing out the raft was over many hours later, I was exhausted. I rested on my knees; my head lowered, and closed my eyes for a few seconds. And then there was another deafening roar. From my kneeling position I went spinning like a Catherine wheel as the raft smashed down on top of me. I was fighting for air again, in a tangled confusion of bodies, arms and legs. Shit! Shit! Not now, we've just finished, I cried to myself, as the roaring wave passed over us. I couldn't believe it.

We struggled through the ordeal yet again, falling asleep on our knees and jerking awake to continue the relentless sponging. Sophie, Daniel, Sophie, Daniel. For the first time we stopped short, leaving water slopping around the bottom of the raft, too spent to finish cleaning it out. We collapsed in a heap and slept, curled up in the pools of water. I couldn't take it any longer.

At the first faint light of dawn we struggled to our knees. I said to Steve, "We've got to get the water out. I'm freezing." This time we did a thorough job, getting rid of every last drop. That was much better. Lying in pools of seawater was fucked. I wrung out my sodden jumper and pulled on my sock and hood, and we both cuddled up trying to get warm as the temperature rose with the dawning day. There was nothing to do but just lie there and conserve our energy. There was no spare energy to even talk. Talking meant shouting over the roar of the storm and was too much of an effort.

I lay there with my thoughts; the EPIRB had been plaguing my mind. How stupid was I, how irresponsible was I, and was I to blame for our predicament? I was filled with recrimination and guilt, until it became too much; I had to turn my thoughts elsewhere. Today we'll be rescued; today we'll be saved, I told myself.

When we stirred around midday, I noticed I wasn't springing to my knees any more, that my movements had become a lot slower. I opened the canopy for a look around. Even more so than yesterday, the sea had grown quieter and the wind had died down to maybe twenty-five knots. From horizon to horizon there was nothing in sight, not even a bird. There were just our fish, their tails wagging as they followed behind the raft. I closed the flaps and rested against the side of the raft, which I noticed had become a bit soft. I felt the sides, pushing them in, and a surge of fear went through me. The raft had definitely lost air. "Shit Steve, the raft is a bit soft mate," I said.

After a bit of a prod, he agreed. We went for the manual refill point located in the corner of the raft and removed the screw-on cap. "Well we have no pump, so we'll have to try with our mouths," I said. Steve said that he would go first and lay down and covered the valve with his mouth. I heard a tiny hiss as the one-way valve operated. "Yeah, I think I got some in," said Steve. He had indeed, and a few minutes later we were satisfied the raft was nice and rigid. Steve screwed the cover back on and sat up, red in the face and breathing hard. "Bit of an effort, mate," he said.

I grimaced. We had used up more energy. Steve said he wanted to wash the mucus out of his mouth, the result of all his straining at the valve. He opened the flaps and started rinsing his mouth. When he had finished I noticed that as he took one, maybe two, mouthfuls of sea water and put them to his mouth, he didn't spit them out. I asked, "You're drinking sea water, are you mate?" and he replied, "Just a couple of drops can't hurt me."

"It's no good for you," I said and left it at that, but I knew it was a bad sign. We were seriously thirsty. Five days without a drop of water or a bite to eat, with our target still eight days away. Boy, things were going to get tough.

As if on cue, Steve said, "I'm going to drink some more piss". He unscrewed the handle and knelt with the paddle blade between his legs. I watched as he retched through the procedure, while struggling with my own thoughts; was urine bad for me? It was waste, after all. I did not know the answer but logic told me it was not right putting all those toxins and chemicals back into my body. I would have to use much more water to get rid of them again. But thirst and the unknown made my decision for me – I would give it a go.

When Steve had finished I said, "Give me that thing. I'm going to have a go." I rinsed the paddle over the side of the raft and struggled to lower my wet jeans while balancing on my knees. Shit, where's my dick? My dick was all shrivelled up – it was difficult, holding the paddle in one hand and my rather dubious member in the other. I aimed at the one-inch opening while being bounced around on my knees, the raft in violent motion. Piss went everywhere. I managed to get some in and then with difficulty, stopped the flow. If I looked at it too long I wouldn't do it, so there was no point holding on to it, I told myself. I blocked my nose and swallowed –

I heaved and heaved again, bile rising in my throat and the taste and smell of urine filled my mouth. I forced it down, burping up the foul gases and heaving and dry retching. Fuck that, no way man; I'm not drinking anymore piss, I said to myself as I rinsed my mouth out with sea water. I handled the paddle to Steve and said, "Here, you can have this. I'm not drinking any more of that shit, not for now, anyway."

"Fair enough," he said, as he stowed the paddle away at the side of the raft.

We decided to sponge the raft out to get rid of the spilt piss and water that had sprayed in over the past few hours. As I leant forward to squeeze out my sponge I noticed a trail of tiny objects trailing away from the raft. What's that? I asked myself. Plankton? Fish eggs? Looking closer, I scooped up a handful of the closest ones; shit, it was tiny pieces of sponge. For the first time I looked closely at the state of my sponge and felt a stab of fear. The sponge was half its original size and starting to disintegrate. Thousands and thousands of squeezes had taken their toll; it was not designed for this continual use. What would we do without sponges? They were our lifeline. If we couldn't get the water out of the raft we would die in no time at all; we would die of hypothermia during the night. I decided not to say anything to Steve.

We lay back down on our backs and stretched out. I counted the waves again, the frequency of breakers was way down; maybe the next few hours would be okay, I thought. But shit I was thirsty and I was hungry. I started thinking about food and water – how much longer could I really go on? My first thoughts of dying crept into my mind; for the first time in my life I started to think that I might die – soon. No, that wasn't possible, it was out of the question, inconceivable, not in the plan at all; but here I was in the middle of the South China Sea, exhausted, thirsty, hungry, wet and getting weaker by the minute, lying in a half-deflated raft with only two disintegrating sponges, a small safety knife and a paddle, alone in the ocean in a storm, away from the shipping lanes. No one was searching for us, nobody knew we were here. I had to face it, things weren't looking good.

I said to Steve, "If I die you can eat me, okay?" We both propped ourselves up on one elbow and looked at each other.

Steve said, "I was having the same thoughts mate."

I said, "Seriously, don't waste me – eat me. I won't feel a thing. I'll be gone, fucked, dead. No point in both of us dying."

Steve replied, "No worries, and you can do the same."

We shook hands on it and lay back down. We had just calmly agreed to eat each other, a totally hideous, unnatural and taboo subject, scorned and repulsed by all the peoples of the world. It was seriously off limits and yet we had discussed it and decided to do it, as easily as if we were ordering breakfast in a greasy fish and chip shop. Strange how things affect you, I thought to myself. My mind was getting clogged with all the issues spinning around my head, to which I had now added death and cannibalism. But

I didn't want to die, I had to stay positive, I had to keep struggling to survive. I pushed this jumble of thoughts to the back of my mind and concentrated on the now.

I was by this time measuring my life in days; I had given myself ten days from day three on the raft to make land, thirteen days in all, with no food or water. It was a big ask but I had set my sights high. Our only other hope was to be rescued by a passing ship. I had ruled out being spotted by a plane; the cloud cover was solid and nearly on the deck, so that was going to be impossible. Our only hope was to be seen by a vessel during daylight, but for this to happen I had to survive the nights to have any chance of living the next day, the next day, and the next day, step by step. All I could do was to take one step at a time. I had to live through another night, I told myself. I was determined I wasn't going to die. I mentally checked myself over again. Sure I was aching all over, I was cold, I was wet, hungry and thirsty; but I definitely wasn't going to keel over yet. I pulled up my jumper and looked at my tummy; fair enough, the reasonably tight bump of my belly had become flatter and softer, but it was sort of still there though. I gave it a friendly pat and it wobbled back. I noticed more red spots and they were bigger, I frowned as I pulled my jumper back down. I lay there and relaxed my breathing, breathing slowly, conserving my energy and trying to meditate and clear my mind of all its tormented thoughts. I focused on one thought: survive the night, survive the night. The afternoon slipped past.

Day 6
Hunger

We went through our usual preparation for the night, thoroughly sponging the raft and removing the afternoon's spray, reaching under the double bottom and drying out that hard-to-get-to and troublesome pool of water. Using our knee pressure to guide the water into little pools that we could soak up, my hands and knees were getting very sore, cramped and raw.

I had a good look around outside but it was the same as always, nothing but the fish and an empty, grey rolling sea. I felt a huge pang of desolation. We were cut off from the rest of the world, devoid of all comforts and necessities of life, completely and utterly alone. Not another soul on the planet knew of our desperate plight. With a heavy heart I slowly closed the canopy and wrapped myself up for the night. We tried to sleep, waiting for what the night would bring. I tried to clear my brain but some thoughts would not go away. This was real, we were here, this was not a dream, this was reality; the dark thoughts were active and were becoming unstoppable. Then exhaustion took over and I drifted off to sleep.

I awoke to a mighty roar all around me and instantly tensed my body and gulped air into my lungs. The raft seemed to fall through the water and started to spin wildly, but didn't capsize this time. It sped over the water, the floor of the raft bouncing and shaking as if on a bed of turbulent air. I held my breath as the raft sped on. About six or seven seconds later it was over. The roar diminished and the raft settled down to its normal motion.

"What the hell was that?" Steve demanded. We were both up on our knees, shaking with the after effects of fear and adrenalin, shocked expressions on our faces. I quickly worked out what had happened. The raft had crested a wave at the precise time that the monster broke. We had surfed on the back of the white water. "Fuck! That was a wild ride! We must have travelled a hundred metres," I said. It felt like that anyway.

"Wild all right," Steve agreed.

We regained our composure, happy that we hadn't capsized and quickly sponged out the little bit of water that had sprayed in. Cuddled back up together I listened to and counted waves. The count was slow; the sea was definitely backing down. This could only mean one thing…the wind was easing! As much as my tortured body begged for respite my brain told me differently. We needed the wind. We really needed the wind. If our progress stopped we would be dead men, floating in a motionless ocean. Not much point to being comfortable then. As much as we hated and feared the capsizings and swampings, and the torturous hours of bailing with our sponges, we needed the wind. Blow, you bastard, blow, I called silently to the heavens.

I did some quick calculations to estimate how far we had travelled. We were coming up to six days on the raft and had travelled maybe three hundred and fifty nautical miles. It could even be as much as four hundred. I opened my imaginary chart in my mind. We had to be halfway across the South China Sea. This was an encouraging thought. Come on, you can do it, I urged myself. Six days! Surely we must now be posted as missing; surely a search would be underway. I closed my eyes thinking these thoughts. We were halfway to Vietnam. Tomorrow we would be rescued; just live, just live – don't ever give up.

We were swamped a couple of times during the night, rudely and cruelly awoken by the cold sea water jetting over our sleeping bodies. Every time, without hesitation, we struggled to our sponging positions on our knees, side-by-side in the middle of the raft, and bailed out the water. No matter how exhausted I felt, no matter how much I just wanted to collapse where I knelt, I made myself repeat the routine as often as was needed.

At daybreak the next morning I slowly gained consciousness as minuscule rays of heat warmed my freezing body. I lay there shivering, not moving, cuddled up close to Steve, conserving every drop of energy that I could. I thought about whether we might make land; we had to do it, it was our main hope. I knew from first-hand experience and my knowledge of the world's geology that most of the oceans' coastlines are guarded by towering cliffs, rocks, razor-sharp coral and outlying reefs, and it was unlikely that we would just peacefully drift ashore on a white, sandy beach like in a scene from the movies. In fact, the opposite was far more likely, that we'd be smashed and torn apart as we were hurled against rocks and coral. Even if we were lucky enough to drift on to an ocean beach, the storm waves and surf would create a formidable barrier. It was a bleak prospect, having so far survived the unspeakable only to be drowned and cut to ribbons on a hostile, rocky coast. I shuddered at the thought. I forced my mind to go blank. It was no good worrying about it yet; we still had a long way to go. My only aim was simply to survive each day, day-by-day, night-by-night, and step-by-step. It was as far as I could let my thoughts take me. I decided not to share my thoughts and fears about the possible landfall with Steve. We needed encouragement and positive thoughts. Our situation was bad enough already and I didn't need to make it worse by pointless scaremongering.

Boy, I was really thirsty and hungry now. Six days without a drop to drink or a morsel to eat. How much longer could we last? I thought about my darling, beloved children. How could I let them down? I could not face the possibility of never seeing them again. I had to live, I just had to. It was too upsetting; I had to push these thoughts away.

I started thinking about food and water, which easily took over in my starved mind and body, even though it was a type of mental torture. Fantasising about food and water was becoming my only way of dealing with the other more hideous devilry that was trying to invade my mind. I settled down with bowls full of trifle, and glasses brimming with ice cold Fanta. I lay there drifting off with my fantasies, when over the never-ending sounds of the sea and the wind I detected a new and unfamiliar sound. Somebody was throwing sand against the canopy. And then it registered.

"Rain! Rain!" I cried to Steve. He also had heard it, and we fumbled with the canopy and stuck our heads out. A light, misty rain was slanting into our faces. We were so excited and for the first time in six days smiles lit up our faces. This was the best thing, the only good experience to have happened since the sinking. We knelt at the opening with our mouths open. But the rain was only heavy enough to wet our faces and our mouths, and there was nothing to swallow. As quickly as it started it stopped. It was a mixture of excitement and disappointment. "Oh, shit! That felt good," I said to Steve as I licked my lips.

"Bloody oath," he replied and added, "I hope there's more where that came from."

"Where there's smoke there's fire," I said. "Let's hope for the best." I scanned the horizon and sure enough, the clouds were darker and here and there, far away, I could see faint misty veils of rain. As we were both awake and up, we sponged out the raft and made ourselves as comfortable as we could. We lay back down in our day positions, stretched out on our backs with our legs resting on the raft buoyancy ring. We both prayed for rain, and a little later it happened again – a light pattering on the raft canopy. We lurched and struggled to our knees and opened the flaps, but before we got our heads out it had stopped.

"Shit," I said, and slumped back down. "We're going to have to be patient; sooner or later we will get a decent rain." This event now fully occupied my mind. Rain, rain, rain – it must rain. All other thoughts had been pushed aside.

Steve was at the opening, rinsing his mouth. This time three or four scoops of sea water were not spat out. "You shouldn't really do that mate, besides it will rain soon," I said, repeating my warning of yesterday.

"It's nothing mate, just a couple of drops. It won't hurt me."

I knew differently but decided to let it drop. Besides, I could not order him to stop. It was a worrying thought though, as I recalled the stories I had read about the effects of drinking sea water. Whatever the circumstances, if you drank too much you went crazy, mad, and then you died. It was as simple as that. There was no way I was going to swallow a drop of it.

Steve had propped himself at the opening searching the clouds for rain. I was resting on my back relaxing, not moving, conserving energy; always conserving energy. The rain started again, and this time it sounded a bit heavier. I clambered up and looked out and yes, this time it was heavier. We opened our mouths and a few drops splashed inside, but it was no good. What could we do? We grabbed the top of the canopy and dragged it down, trying to pool the water in the indentation we had made. But it didn't work for two reasons. The slanting of the wind-driven rain seemed to pass clear over us, with not much at all landing on the canopy and what little that did was too salty to drink, far too salty, and I spat out the tiny amount that I had in my mouth. The rain had washed the salt off the encrusted canopy and it had mixed with the water and made it undrinkable. We had to figure out something else.

We let go of the canopy and it snapped back into shape. There was a small v-shaped gutter built into the back of the canopy facing away from the wind. Attached to this was a black rubber drinking tube, hanging on the inside of the raft. This must have been an afterthought by the raft designers and it was simply ineffective. Positioned on the wrong side of the raft, not a single drop issued from the tube. What were we going to do? We had nothing to catch or store water in. And then the rain stopped. "Shit!" I said again, in desperate frustration. What were we going to do? I lay back down and collected my thoughts. Regardless of everything that had gone on, I stuck rigidly to my routine; keeping covered, staying as dry as I could and relaxing, conserving energy. I didn't get to lie there for long.

"Look out mate!" Steve cried out. He was still on his knees at the opening and was grabbing at the useless deflated upper ring of the raft and pulling it up, as a breaking wave slammed into us. Steve's effort had saved us from what would have been a major swamping. But even so, a few buckets full of water sprayed inside.

"Shit," I said again and struggled to my knees, drenched. "Let's get this water out." I reached for my sponge in my jeans and looked at it. It was finished; just a small useless piece of squashed foam. "Fuck me, my sponge has had it," I said to Steve.

Steve looked at his, saying, "So is mine. What are we going to do?" There was only one answer and I was already prepared for this event. "We need your singlet, mate," I said.

He didn't complain or argue. It was all we had left to use. He stripped off his vest and took off his singlet, tore it in half and gave me a piece. I wrapped it around the remains of my sponge and started the job. It wasn't too bad, it got the water out. When we'd finished I tied my piece of singlet safely to one of the grab lines on the inside of the raft, and put the little piece of foam in my pocket.

Then we heard it again, starting with the same soft pattering and then increasing in strength. We lurched to the opening side by side. Water was running down the side of the canopy on our side. I craned my neck around and started licking the small trickles of water. Shit! I spat. It was still salty. I rubbed my hands over the canopy trying to wash the salt off. I tried again and yes, it was definitely better but still salty, but I didn't need to spit it out. I wasn't getting far just licking at the drops so in desperation I grabbed hold of the canopy on the inside and dragged it down, forming a valley between the canopy and the inflation ring of the raft. Water started pooling. I leaned out of the raft even further and stuck my head into the valley I had created and forcing my head to the bottom, I sucked. A small mouthful of water, glorious beautiful water! Steve quickly followed suit and I cried out in rapture, "I got a mouthful, I got a mouthful!"

"So did I!" replied Steve.

The rain was still falling and I went again, another mouthful and another, and another. Then the rain stopped suddenly; it was like turning off a tap. I didn't care; I was in heaven. "I got four mouthfuls, man," I said breathlessly to Steve.

"Me too, I got the same, four!" he replied, a huge smile on his face.

"Oh shit, that feels good, man. Man that is good," I said.

The effect of four small mouthfuls of fresh water, not even half a cup, was huge. We were rapt, lying on our backs as content as if we had just finished Christmas dinner. We talked and chatted away, the first real conversation we had had since getting on the raft. We had worked out a system for getting drinking water, which would work perfectly and be fair. We would each have one side of the canopy on the side exposed to the weather, where we would be able to collect an equal amount of water. If it rained again we would be ready. We lay and waited, our hopes renewed.

Later in the afternoon it rained again, not as hard this time, but enough to get two small mouthfuls of sweet water. It had given me enough strength, if only in my mind, to live through to the next day. I was going to survive the night. I was going to take another step forward.

Day 7
Rain

Six small gulps of water had felt great. It didn't matter how much benefit it did our bodies or how much longer it would help us live, it was the psychological effect that was huge. Something really good had happened when so far it had been all bad: the sinking, the capsizing, losing everything; the ships, plane and oil rigs at night; the mind and body-breaking effort of staying alive. It had all been bad. In fact, so far it had been a nightmare; a living nightmare, our bodies and souls tortured.

We made our preparations for the night in good spirits, eagerly looking forward to more rain. The weather and the sea had changed. The wind was still blowing at about twenty-five to thirty knots, steady but not gusting. The only gauge I had for the wind's direction was to estimate the position of the rising and setting sun. I mean estimating, for the cloud cover was total and complete. I sat for ages staring at the horizon, trying to figure the pattern of light as dawn rose and dusk fell. The fading light was in its familiar position. If anything, we were more westing. The clouds themselves were thicker and darker and the sea had become peakier. It appeared that the effects of two different weather systems or currents had collided. There was a clear second sea running across the line of waves we were accustomed to. This broke up the line of the sea and diminished the number of large, breaking waves. It was, however, very confused with dangerous peaks and troughs, and the raft was being pushed and shoved from two directions. I said to Steve, "Let's try something different tonight."

"What do you have in mind?" he asked.

From what I had noticed earlier in the day, I suggested that we try a change of positions. Instead of lying along the raft like matches in a matchbox, I would sit in the middle and face the canopy opening. I stretched my legs out and put them on the inflated ring next to the entry and leant back, my head resting on the ring on the other side. I wriggled my feet under the deflated upper ring and then twisted them so they were pointing up. This pushed the upper ring up, giving us another ten inches of freeboard. I then grabbed hold of the canvas webbing of the internal boarding ladder and pulled back. This held the upper ring locked firmly in place, held up by my feet. Now the bottom of the Velcro-closed canopy opening was on the outside of the raft. Any water or spray hitting the canopy would be directed back into the sea and not into the raft. I resembled a water skier about to be pulled out of the water. "Okay. Get comfy next to me, mate," I said to Steve.

He cuddled up good and close and with a bit of wriggling and arranging we were as comfortable as we could get. Our weight was now concentrated at the back of the raft. Before, we had chosen to lay the other way to try to keep the weight forward, counteracting the force of the waves that were lifting and capsizing us. This new position felt a bit strange because we had become used to our routine, but I was interested to see what would happen. I tested my new charge. Leaning back and pulling hard on the boarding ladder and raising my legs, I raised the front of the raft slightly out of the water.

"I'll take first watch," I said to Steve. I actually chuckled. Drinking fresh water had definitely helped my mood.

"No worries mate, give us a nudge when you need a spell," Steve replied. I arranged my hood and pulled my jumper up around my ears and rested my head on the inflated ring. Not too bad, I thought. My legs were up and stretched out, even though my joints were becoming very sore, especially my knees. Imagine kneeling on a wildly moving waterbed trying to keep upright for six days non-stop, because that was what it had been like. I rested my hands over my groin, arms over my chest and relaxed, my eyes closed but not sleeping, conserving my energy and waiting to see what would happen next. Listening to the sea, I prayed for more rain. We had grown accustomed to the noise of the rushing, breaking waves, and recognising which ones would hit and those that would miss. Eventually I heard the familiar roar. Steve flinched in his sleep as I pulled back hard and lifted my legs. The breaking wave struck us hard and passed under us, surging the raft forward as it rode on the white water. I was rapt.

"Man, did you feel that? That one would have got us before," I said to Steve, who was by now wide-awake. At the very least we would have been badly swamped, there was no doubt about it. I knew my waves. Only a few cups full of water had squirted in. I couldn't believe it; we had saved ourselves hours of gruelling work and from being saturated in cold seawater. How much energy must we have saved? Excellent! Excellent, I thought to myself. But was it just a fluke or a lucky strike? I settled back and waited. Twice more I heard the roar, and twice more I leaned back and pulled, raising my legs with the same result as before; the white water rushing under the raft and pushing us on. Oh, this was just great, just great, I congratulated myself. This was definitely the way to go. I thought about the hundreds of times we would have had to mop the water out with a little piece of cotton rag, balancing on our knees, saturated, cold and tired. We had had a good day – a small drink of water and we had worked out how to operate the raft.

I stayed in this position for as long as I could until my legs could take it no longer. I asked Steve if he wanted to have a go for a while. "No worries," he replied. We shuffled around and changed positions. Steve locked himself in, his feet holding up the deflated ring and his shoulders pushed into the back of the raft, pulling on the boarding ladder. "Okay mate, cuddle up," he said.

We settled in again and this time I tried to sleep. I don't know how long I slept before I was woken by the sound of another rushing wave. My body instantly tensed, fear ripping through me as I took a deep breath. But Steve did the job, lifting his legs, pulling and leaning back, as the wave hit and passed under us, taking the raft with it. This was too good to be true, I thought. So far only a few cups full of water had entered the raft all night. With our newfound confidence it was easy to get back to sleep. I stirred a few times as the raft bucked and surged but before I knew it I felt the warmth of day creeping into the raft, and knew I had survived another night.

Today we will be rescued; today it must rain, I thought to myself, as I came slowly to my senses. I propped myself up on one elbow and struggled to my knees. We opened the canopy and started our morning chore of mopping and drying out the inside of the raft. The remains of our sponges had long gone and we were left with only our two pieces of cotton singlet. I had been concentrating so much on the inside of the raft and the slopping water that I had barely glanced outside. When I did I got a bit of a surprise; the water was brown, almost muddy. "Shit look at the water," I said to Steve.

He was soon kneeling next to me at the opening. "Looks a bit dirty, no tuna in that lot," he said, with an attempt at a bit of humour.

When searching for these great beasts we looked for crystal clear water; I called it white water, and Steve was right, this was not tuna water. I looked about and saw a large piece of bamboo, waterlogged and floating barely a few wavelengths away. There were small pieces of vegetation, plastic and other rubbish all around. Then two brilliant white terns splashed past the raft, skimming and dancing over the waves – the classic telltale signs of land – dirty water, flotsam and birds. My mind raced. Where were we? Even at best speed we could not have made it to Vietnam; no way, I told myself. With the westing that I was sure we were making, it could only mean one thing – Hainan Island. But where was it? To our side or in front of us? I shuddered involuntarily as the thoughts of waves crashing against rocky cliffs flashed through my mind. We both searched the horizon in front of us and pulled down the canopy to see ahead, but there was nothing but grey clouds and the heaving ocean.

"We must be close to Hainan Island," I told Steve. "I don't know where it is but that must be it, there's no other answer. And that's good," I reassured him, "It means we are still on course and on schedule to get to Vietnam. We must be close to two-thirds of the way there."

I drew again from my memory of the chart of the South China Sea. We must be at least two-thirds of the way, I reassured myself. I scanned the sky behind us. The clouds were thick and dark in a few places, with curtains of misty grey draping down to the ocean. More rain; maybe today we might get another drink. We closed up and made ourselves comfy, this time resuming the same positions as the night before: one man protecting us from the sea, the other curled up resting, next to him. A couple of times more through the morning this practice paid off, saving us from being swamped and drenched, our raft-veteran status raising a notch. We were getting to know our little home better and better. We lay there waiting, resting.

"Fuck, I'm thirsty mate. I hope we get some rain today," said Steve.

"Me too," I replied.

I was getting weaker, every movement took more effort, took more time. I closed my eyes and tried to rest. Seven days and only half a cup of water, how much longer could my body take it? After a while the pattering started again and we were instantly alert, struggling for the canopy opening, but it stopped just as quickly as it started. We stuck our heads out, but there was no rain in sight. I looked forward; a small misty dark cloud was racing away. "That's it, may as well lie back down," I said to Steve.

Before we did I again noticed Steve taking a few handfuls of sea water and putting them to his mouth. Damn, I thought to myself, this was not good. The urge to drink was taking control of our minds. I decided not to say anything. I had already warned him twice. I felt the sides of the raft and they were getting spongy again. "My turn, I'd better get some air into this thing before we sink," I said to Steve.

I unscrewed the valve cap and lay on my stomach. Covering the valve with my mouth, I took a deep breath and puffed. I felt a tiny amount of air pass through the tight non-return valve. Phew, this was going to take some effort. I took another big breath and after what seemed like an age I lay panting on my back on the bottom of the raft. The flotation ring was tight and I was buggered. As I lay there recovering my breath it started to rain again. Steve was quickly up and looking outside. I still lay there panting, waiting. I had already thought about the procedure; we had to let sufficient rain fall to rinse the salt off the canopy, which was constantly being sprayed and splashed by the turbulent sea. Once again the pattering stopped as abruptly as it had started and I was glad I'd saved myself the effort of battling to my knees again. "Shit," said Steve as he closed up the canopy, his disappointment palpable.

I told him we would have to wait until the rain got heavier and washed off the salt. No point wasting energy jumping up every time it started. Steve saw the logic in this and agreed, and we lay there waiting. Twice more the rain started and we forced ourselves to stay where we were. The urge to grab for the opening was overwhelming; equally as overwhelming as our desire to drink. Twice more the rain stopped, the fine pattering turning off like a tap. The third time the rain was a bit heavier and we counted the seconds, holding our breath. "Fuck this, I'm getting out there," said Steve.

The urge got the better of me and the thought of missing out was unthinkable, so I followed him up. This time it was still raining when we opened the flaps and I made my hollow in the canopy and sticking my head in, I slurped and spat. Shit, salty, way too salty. The rain stopped. "Damn and shit!" I cursed. I searched the horizon in the direction of the weather and there were still more rain squalls about. I said to Steve, "Look, there's more rain coming, we just have to be patient. Sooner or later we will get a decent lot."

Steve had seen the rain squalls too and nodded. Dejectedly, we closed the canopy and resumed our positions and waited. Another start and another stop, and then another start and another stop. Our minds and bodies were being tortured. My mind was screaming at the heavens: rain, rain, rain, *please*, we need rain! It started again, the same soft pattering. We waited, and the beating intensified. We held our breath as agonising seconds passed, and the rain grew even stronger.

With the same "Fuck this!" Steve was up and opening the canopy.

By the time I was on my knees the noise of the wind-driven rain was nearly deafening. My heart racing, I pushed my head outside; we were in a downpour, the horizon blackened by the driving rain. I furiously wiped my hands over the side of the canopy where the water was running down in tiny streams. With one hand clutching the canopy and pulling it down, the other arm across my chest and holding up the deflated ring, I formed my pool and stuck my head in and sucked. Oh yes! A small mouthful of sweet, fresh water ran down my throat. Again, again and again I swallowed, the rain still belting down. I stopped for a few seconds, my heart pumping hard as I watched as a small pool of water reformed in the hollow. I waited for as long as I could bear, fearing being thrown off balance or a wave slopping in and losing the precious liquid. I plunged my face back down in the water and it covered my mouth. I counted as I filled my mouth and swallowed seven consecutive huge mouthfuls of water. When I raised my head to take a breath, tears were running down my face. I cried to Steve, "I got seven mouthfuls at a go, mate! Oh shit it's beautiful."

Steve was busy on his side of the raft but managed to answer, "Me too mate. Fuck this feels good! God this feels good!"

More water had gathered in my hollow, formed by my vice-like grip, and I bent my head and drank again and again. We were both bending, our bodies twisting as far as they could outside of the raft to put our heads down to drink, oblivious of the crashing waves that threatened to throw us off balance and throw us out of the raft or swamp us. We had only one overriding urge, to drink as much water as we possibly could. The rain stopped abruptly and I sucked up my last mouthful. I had counted twenty-eight mouthfuls. *Twenty-eight*! I was beside myself. I felt bloated and light-headed and unable to fit in another drop. I let out a huge belch; releasing all of the air I had gulped down with the water, and collapsed into the raft laughing. We both lay there laughing. What a feeling, what a beautiful feeling! I could not believe that a small drink of water could give me so much pleasure. I could easily take one more step; I could easily live through the next night. I said to Steve, "Bloody oath that feels good mate. I feel good."

"Me too, mate," he replied.

I retreated into my thoughts and slept, my tummy full of water. The sky began to darken as we started our eighth day on the raft.

Day 8
Entering Hell

We happily prepared ourselves for the eighth night on the raft. The fresh water had done wonders for our spirits and we were also happy that we hadn't been capsized or swamped for over twenty-four hours. The fear and the shock of being dunked into the cold sea, the battle to right the raft and struggle back into it, and the mind-numbing task of emptying the raft with a shred of singlet was complete torture, and had sucked the energy from us, leaving us totally exhausted. Thanks to our new system in the life raft, we had now been spared this torment for over twenty-four hours and we finally felt as though we were in control of the raft, and it was a good feeling. We dried up thoroughly and secured the canopy.

"I'll take first watch," I said, smiling to Steve. We settled down to endure a night bumping and rocking westward in the darkness, riding with the storm. During my watch deep into the night, I heard a familiar roar. It sounded like a freight train and it was going to hit us, and hit us hard. I pulled back with all my might but this time there was nothing I could do to stop the impact of the wave hitting us. One quick gasp for air and we were engulfed again, flipping over in the churning sea.

It was a shock being thrown back into the water after thirty-six hours or so. I closed my eyes and let out a silent wail, knowing what was coming next – hours of coldness and wetness, balancing on my knees, clearing the water out of the raft. But that was all the self-pity I would allow myself. We just had to get on with it. If we stayed where we were, unable to cope with the task, we would be dead from the cold within a few hours.

We struggled with the raft in the stormy sea. We had grown weaker now and the process took longer than it had before. Cold, soaked and exhausted, we pulled ourselves back into the raft, which had filled up with water. I lowered my head and closed my eyes. How much more of this could I really take? It wasn't my mind that was giving up, it was my body.

"Where's my sponge, see my sponge anywhere?" Steve called in the darkness. We still called our pieces of singlet sponges. I felt all around and under the double bottom as Steve did the same, but it was nowhere to be found, it was gone. "Shit!" was all I could say. I looked down at my piece of frayed rag and then, tearing it in half, handed a scrap to Steve. Side by side on our cramped, sore knees, we began. There was only one way that I could cope with the ordeal by this stage. I dipped the small shred of cotton into the water and reaching out through the opening to squeeze out the water, began to mentally chant: one handful for Sophie, one handful for Daniel . . . Sophie . . . Daniel . . . over and over in my mind. Steve and I worked in silence, each in our own private hell. We worked at a slow, steady pace, never varying the rhythm of our movements, and continued without stopping or hesitating until the raft was dry. My mind and body had become numb, and all I wanted to do was curl up and sleep where I knelt.

I shook my head to clear my exhaustion. We had to get back into position to prevent any further capsizing. I didn't want to go through that again. Not tonight, please, I begged in my mind. Don't let that happen again tonight. It was Steve's turn at the controls and after he got himself into position I cuddled up next to him, my chest against his side and my head buried under his armpit.

I tried to block out my thoughts and the intensifying nightmares that were taking over my mind when I slept. I was in despair, lonely, fearful and totally exhausted and felt as though I was descending into hell. I had fallen into an uneasy sleep when, without warning, we were hit again, this time from below. The force of the impact threw me into the air and then I was falling, the raft seeming to drop into a hole in the ocean and be pulled under. I was terrified. Was this it – sucked into a black hole and drowned in the middle of the night? Sea water poured in, the raft hesitated, and then its buoyancy won the battle and it burst back up to the surface in a welter of foam and bubbles. I was on my knees shaking with fear. "Fuck man, what happened? Fuck that was scary man!" I gasped.

What had happened was that the peaks of two colliding waves had hit us. These peaks climb to twice the height of the surrounding sea and then drop away just as fast, leaving a hole twice as deep. We had been very lucky; any deeper and the sea would have swallowed us. But the raft was flooded again and I moaned inwardly. With the will to live still beating inside me I reached for my rag and started. Sophie, Daniel, Sophie, Daniel. I was still chanting and numb with shock as the light of a new day started to spread across the eastern sky. We had made it through another night.

Before succumbing to my exhaustion, I said to Steve, "Don't worry mate, today we will be rescued."

He replied tersely, "You say that every fucking day."

I closed my eyes, knowing that hell was beckoning me and that there was no escaping it. I slept for an indeterminate time. When I slowly regained consciousness I tried to raise myself up, every movement getting more and more difficult and taking more time. I opened the canopy and looked outside. The sea was back to its normal grey-green, a steady line of breaking waves advancing upon us. The clouds had lifted slightly and were not quite so dark, but it was still blowing at twenty-five to thirty knots and there was nothing else in sight. Even the fish that had been our only companions for the last seven days were gone. It occurred to me that they didn't like the dirty water. I fumbled to close the Velcro fastenings; the job was getting harder and harder. Starting at the top and working my way down, I was almost at the bottom when a gust of wind pulled the Velcro apart again. I started again, concentrating on the Velcro, when

I realised what the problem was. There were tiny brown hairs entwined and matted into the Velcro, rendering it all but useless. I plucked out a tiny fibre and saw that it was from my jumper. On the countless times that I had squeezed out the sponge and clambered back into the raft, my jumper must have rubbed against the Velcro, depositing fibres each time. I picked and scratched at the hairs, but it was useless. The Velcro was hopelessly clogged.

I lay back down and rested my aching and cramped legs on the side of the raft, which I noticed was starting to feel soft under my heels. I reached over and felt the inflation ring. Shit, I said to myself, if it was not one thing it was another. Now the raft was losing air and starting to buckle and bend with every wave that passed under or slammed into it. The raft had taken a flogging over the past week, pounded relentlessly by thousands of hammering waves, and the wear on it was becoming all too apparent. The corner seams were becoming unglued and starting to open up, and there was fraying and signs of stress everywhere I looked. This frightened me – which would last longer, the raft or us? The certainty of our fate if the raft collapsed was that we'd be alone, paddling for our lives in an angry sea, waiting for the end. Please not that way; please not that way, I begged in my mind. I tried to remain positive but our situation was getting desperate. We'd only had half a raft to start with, and now it was beginning to fail completely. On top of that, we only had half a singlet and one paddle, and only a few mouthfuls of water and nothing to eat in eight days. How much longer could we go on?

Steve was awake and resting on his back. "We'd better get some air into this baby before we end up swimming to Vietnam," I said to him.

"My turn," he replied, and crawled into position. While he was busy huffing and puffing at the valve, I studied the canopy opening. There were small eyelets in the canopy with rings attached to the deflated upper ring, securing the grab lines to the outside of the raft. I took the safety knife out of its pocket, cut lengths of the heaving line and with a bit of effort, succeeded in lashing the canopy firmly closed. Steve finished blowing up the raft and it wasn't a bad result at all. The inflation ring felt tight again and my lashing of the canopy had actually lifted the deflated ring up and made the whole raft feel even more secure.

I looked over at Steve who was looking gaunt. Hundreds of small red sores covered his exposed arms and his jeans were torn to ribbons up to his knees. "Your jeans are rooted," I said to him.

"Yeah, I know," he replied, and started to tear off the ribbons of rotting denim, exposing his legs which were covered in more red sores. I decided to check myself over and pulled up the legs of my jeans. First the right leg – holy shit! An angry red line about an inch wide stretched up my shin from my ankle to half way up to my knee. I pulled up the other leg; there was nothing on my shinbone but there was a hole about two inches round which looked as though it was eating into the side of my calf. "Shit!" I said, appalled at the sight of my leg. Everywhere else I looked I was covered in red spots and lumps. I lifted my jumper and my stomach was now concave and covered in the same red sores. I probed my legs, feeling for the muscles, but they were gone. Instead, small sacks of jelly in wrinkled, loose skin, hung down in folds. I was wasting away. I was shocked and repulsed by the sight of my own body. It was unrecognisable. It wasn't mine.

I started to panic. Was I really going to die, just waste away, consumed from within, unable to fight it? This thought was more than I could cope with and I used the only means I knew to push these tortured thoughts from my mind. I thought about food, beautiful food, and focused on the first mouthful of trifle I would have. I was starving to death and I couldn't stop thinking about food.

After a while my thoughts turned to Steve lying next to me. He had agreed to let me eat him if he died and I had said the same to him. But whatever happened, I was determined to outlive him. In my ravaged state, my thoughts began to travel along what I assumed to be a logical course; if Steve died first, I would eat him. If I ate him it would give me the strength I would need to make it to Vietnam and safety. 'Live' took on a whole new meaning: to survive, all I had to do was outlive Steve and eat him. It was obvious. Anyone would have arrived at the same conclusion, I told myself. The perversity and bleakness of these thoughts never occurred to me, such was the state of my starved and tortured mind.

I set about making plans for what I would do when Steve died, as calmly as if I was organising a school fair. First of all I would have to catch him quickly; a problem that I set aside for the moment. I would have to catch him fast because first I would need his blood. To get it, I would puncture his jugular vein with the knife and suck out as much blood as possible before his body went cold and his blood congealed. Then using the knife, I would open up his belly and eat his liver and kidneys, setting aside his stomach and intestines to be cleaned later. The stomach could be used as a buoyancy bag or water container, and the gut? Who knows? It might come in handy for something. Next I would hack off his head and eat his brains and eyes. I would keep the skull to use as a water bailer, complete with finger holes. Then I would strip as much meat off him as possible and hang this from the canopy in strips to dry. From the bones I would get a good supply of the easily digestible and nourishing marrow and then use them as tools, clubs, spears and hooks. As well as for food, I could also use some of the dried meat as bait. There's quite a bit you can get from a dead body, I thought to myself. There was no doubt about it, Steve's body would give me all the nourishment I would need to survive for another ten days at least, which would be more than enough to make it to Vietnam, where I was convinced we were headed. Then my last job would be to toss Steve's carcass over the side and clean up the mess. After all, I couldn't live with a dead man lying next to me in the raft for too long.

I was dying of starvation and these thoughts didn't faze me at all. My basic survival instinct had surfaced and taken control of my brain. I had to survive and one way to do that, perhaps the only way, would be to eat Steve. Not once did it occur to me that there was anything repulsive about thinking like this, or to contemplate the consequences of this act. Such thoughts never entered my head. My need to survive dominated my every thought. Everything was now about my surviving.

My grisly planning was interrupted by the sound of rain. Holding my breath, I prayed for the sound to continue but just as we raised ourselves up on our elbows it stopped. "Shit!" said Steve. He got up and untied the canopy and looked around.

"See anything?" I called out. I was lying curled up, conserving my energy.

"No, fuck all. A little bit of rain, a couple of small patches on the horizon, but nothing like yesterday," he said. He took a few swipes of sea water and swallowed them.

"You shouldn't really do that, it's bad for you," I said.

Steve replied angrily, "How the fuck do you know it's bad for me?"

"I've read all about…".

Steve cut me short. "You've read this, you've read that! You reckon you know it all! Just tell me how you really know it's not good for me. I'm still alive, aren't I?"

I couldn't answer him. He was right. I didn't really know. "Okay! Okay. I agree," I said, trying to calm him down.

"I'm going to drink some piss now. I suppose you'll tell me that that's bad for me too, eh?" he came back at me. I said nothing. The fact was, I actually did think drinking urine was bad for us but I couldn't be bothered with a pointless argument. I lay there as he retched through the process.

The tension between us had begun to increase. I was deep in thought when the rain started again, beating a faint tattoo on the canopy. It got heavier and we scrambled for the lashing. My hands were cold and numb, my knuckles red raw from the thousands of times I had pushed them into the rough surface of the double bottom. I fumbled with the small ropes, the rain still coming down. We got ourselves into position and craned our bodies outside. We were in the middle of a small rain squall and I had made my hollow and pushed my head in. I was too quick and eager and spat the first mouthful into the sea in disgust. The next one was better, still a bit salty but I swallowed anyway. Three more drinks and the rain passed over. It was finished. Small as it was, it felt good. "I got four, mate," I said.

"Me too, I got four too," replied Steve.

With all our excitement about having fresh water to drink, our earlier tense moment had disappeared. I sat on the side of the raft and looked around. The ocean was definitely calmer and the wind had eased. There was a lull in the storm.

Inside, the raft smelt of urine. Not just what Steve had spilt but mine as well. All we could do was lie there and piss; the effort of trying to do it over the side was no longer worth the energy that it took. Besides, the warmth of the urine was comforting as it trickled over my legs and thighs.

"Let's leave the canopy open for a while and get rid of some of this stench," I said.

"Yeah mate, good idea. It is a bit on the nose," he replied.

Later in the afternoon another small rain squall passed overhead. That time we got two small mouthfuls each and that made six mouthfuls for the day. It wasn't much but was still something. As the end of the eighth day approached, I knew I would survive another night. And I would outlive Steve and then eat him. I was going to live.

Day 9
The Mako

As the darkness descended all hope of rescue disappeared until morning. I feared and hated the night. After thoroughly drying the raft and tightly lashing the canopy, I painfully and slowly took up my position in the raft, my legs splayed to support the deflated ring, the canvas webbing of the boarding ladder between my legs, and my shoulders pressed firmly into the ring on the opposite side to the opening. "Okay, I'm in, your turn now," I said to Steve.

Soon he was pressed up tightly to my side with one ear turned to the sea. I felt myself drifting off and knocked on the gates of hell. I stumbled down an endless corridor, opening doors as I went. In one room were my children later in life, tears running down their faces as they held an old photo of me, never having known what had happened to their daddy. In another room were my parents, brothers and sisters, all with the same sad expressions on their faces as a question echoed around the room – where are you my son? In another room off the corridor was a judge with a gavel. "Guilty!" he shouted, slamming down his gavel. "For not buying the EPIRB the sentence is death."

In other rooms were more judges. Guilty, guilty, and guilty! They slammed their gavels down. Guilty of murder, guilty of negligence, guilty of greed and foolhardiness. The sentence? Death! I saw my body face down in the water, arms outstretched; visions of me crushed and broken on a rocky ledge, cliffs towering over me; later, my sun bleached bones lying amongst driftwood on an uncharted coral atoll. The torment of the nightmare continued as I lurched blindly down the corridor, and only ended with the sound of rolling thunder. I pulled back, legs raised and fully alert as the waves hit.

Waking was no better than my fevered nightmare, with the renewed realisation of our predicament. Drifting before the storm-lashed ocean I cried inwardly, I don't want to die, I don't want to die, I really don't want to die. There were people who needed me and exciting challenges still to be met. Surely this can't be my time, I am not going to die tonight, no way; I am going to live until morning. Surely we will be saved tomorrow. I just have to hang on and never, ever give up – that was the key. I could end the agony easily, simply give up, or I could take the hard option and withstand this assault against my body and mind and fight to survive. Every minute, every hour, every day gave me a chance to live. And I still had Steve to eat. I tried to remain positive.

I drifted in and out of consciousness; my nightmares intermingled with the prospect of feasting on my mate. Late into the night, we were awoken by the unmistakable sound of rain, but it stopped before we moved. In order to conserve our energy, there was no point in moving until the rain had intensified and held steady for long enough to wash the salt off the canopy. This could take at least a minute of heart-stopping agony while we hoped against hope that the sound would continue. I had to resist my animal instinct, the lust for water, and remain where I was until I was sure the rain would persist. To get up on my knees and open the canopy was becoming an ever-harder chore and burnt precious energy.

"Fuck the rain," Steve said dejectedly.

"I'm about fucked here, do you want to swap for a while?" I asked Steve.

"No worries mate," he replied.

We slowly and painfully swapped places, staggering around on our knees, lurching and tumbling into one another, as the storm tossed and bucked the raft. Steve eventually settled down and I cuddled up nice and close, pressing my body into his. I could instantly feel the warmth that our bodies generated and the small comfort that offered in an ocean of despair.

Freed from the responsibility of driving the raft, I was able to sleep. I needed desperately to sleep. Please let me sleep; please let me escape from this horror, my mind cried out. I did sleep, stirring, flinching and holding my breath as roars of rushing water invaded my stupor. When I regained my senses it was light. I remained motionless, my body aching and cramped. I shivered as I pulled my sodden jumper back over my ears. Another day had started. I had survived another night. We might be saved today, anything could happen. I shuffled myself against Steve and he shuffled back. He had survived another night as well.

We lay there gathering our strength for the chores we needed to perform, our routine. We had to stick rigidly to our jobs, knowing full well that to stop would be the beginning of the end. 'Give up and die' had become imprinted on my mind. I said, "We'd better get this raft cleaned up, mate."

"Yeah, righto," replied Steve. Like a couple of paralytic drunks, we made it to our knees and opened the canopy flaps. Nothing but the heaving sea and grey clouds met my gaze. I felt the sides of the raft and we needed more air already. I said to Steve, "Let's get the water out first and then I'll blow this fucker up."

"No worries, mate," he replied.

It had been a good night really; no capsizings, no swampings. Thank heavens for small mercies, I thought to myself, as I pushed my rag into the rough double bottom and started – Sophie, Daniel, Sophie, Daniel. The water was mixed with our urine and had become thicker and more pungent, the stench of ammonia burning our nostrils. We stuck at it until we had every last drop out. We knew from experience that the dryer the raft, the more comfortable we would be. The more comfortable we were the more energy we would save.

So there was no point in half doing the job. It was not a case of near enough was good enough.

"Okay, now for the air," I said, after I had tied my rag to a grab handle inside the raft. The valve was on Steve's side, and he unscrewed the cap and shuffled out of the way as I lay on my stomach and squirmed my way up to it. I took a deep breath and started to blow. The tiniest hiss of air reached my ears. This was going to be even harder than before; my lungs were getting weaker. I continued until I was dizzy with the effort, breathless, with my heart pounding in my chest. I felt the sides of the raft and they were tight enough. Thank God for that, I thought, as I fought to regain my breath and calm my racing heart. Steve decided to blow up the double bottom and the small air tube that held the canopy in place, something that we had not previously done. I felt them both and they were soft and spongy. "Good idea," I said.

These valves were not as tight as the others and before long Steve had the tubes inflated. It felt a lot better. The main buoyancy chamber was tight, the double bottom firm underneath us and the canopy rigid, the raft dry. I took one last look around before I tied the canopy flaps closed. There was still nothing but the heaving sea. Scanning the horizon as the raft crested the swells, there was not a rain squall in sight.

A movement under the raft suddenly caught my eye. What was that? I peered into the sea, focusing into the depths. There it was again, a grey streak a few dozen metres from the raft, disappearing into the foaming water. I knelt next to the edge of the raft and watched, my heart starting to beat harder, fear clutching my bowels. I recognised it the next time it appeared, there was no mistaking its dorsal fin as it cut the surface and sliced through the water. A mako. I had seen hundreds of them; an old and known foe of the tuna long-liners. Even though a lot smaller than the great whites, in my book they were a lot deadlier. Tough and aggressive, they showed no fear. After having their half-eaten meal taken from them as we landed damaged fish, I have seen makos turn their anger and savagery on a boat, snapping and crunching their teeth into the steel sides. They do not hesitate to attack.

The mako had picked up our scent, the blood from our sores mixing with the water as we sponged it over the side. This was an aggressive killer that was following in our wake, sensing a meal. Fear surged through me again as I thought of the multiple rows of razor sharp, ripping teeth in the mako's gaping jaw. One attack on the raft and we would be torn to pieces, in a foaming red frenzy. I eased myself back under the canopy, trying to hide. Had the mako seen me? I quivered at the thought.

"Anything out there mate?" Steve said, as I lashed the canopy tight.

 "Nothing mate, just the ocean." There was no point in both of us being shit scared, I thought, as I lay down on my back. The effort of drying and pumping up the raft had left me weak, so there was nothing more to do but lie there curled up, and return to my thoughts. To avoid becoming overwhelmed with despair, I turned my thoughts to food again, immersing myself in the fantasy. Every exquisite taste imaginable, every drop of effervescent liquid I could think up, formed in my mind, as the desire for nourishment took control. But eventually tiring of these mind games, I began focusing on the real food issue at hand – the meal that was lying next to me.

This time even more sinister thoughts arose. Would I kill to eat? Would I kill another person to survive? Would I kill Steve? The answer was yes, if I absolutely needed to in order to live. Not from me, Mark Smith, but from another source deep within me. My will to live overpowered everything else. There was no question of compassion, no rational interpretation of such a crime or its consequences; just a perverse fear bordering on obsession – I needed his blood, I would need him hot. If he died in the middle of the night, undetected, he would be of far less value to me than if I was aware of his moment of death, because otherwise I would not get the fluid that I so urgently needed. Having stepped beyond the realms of all rational thought, I was convinced that it was not unreasonable to contemplate what I was considering: I believed that anyone in my position would do the same.

Rain interrupted my thoughts again. I was instantly alert, holding my breath and listening to the rain beat down on the canopy as I ticked off the seconds until I could bear it no longer. I scrambled to the opening and started to unlash the flaps as Steve did the same on the other side. The rain held steady and would be washing off the salt. We thrust our heads and shoulders out, grabbed the canopy from the inside and bent ourselves to the task. Bouncing precariously on our wobbly knees, our heads and shoulders barely inches from the rushing sea, I had completely forgotten about the prowling mako. The rain stopped as suddenly as it had started, as if someone had turned off a tap. "Shit!" I cursed, after only two small swallows. I had needed two hundred but it was better than nothing. The pure, sweet trickle down my throat had been well worth the effort.

I leant back against the raft and started to inspect my legs. Steve was still leaning outside and I noticed him drink more of the sea water, scooping seven quick handfuls into his mouth. I was past remonstrating with him. It was his funeral. Suddenly Steve froze and stared at the sea. "Fucking mako!"

So he had seen it too; it seemed the shark was still stalking its prey. I shuddered as I thought of myself a few seconds ago, inches from its murderous jaws. "Yeah, I saw the fucker before. The bloody thing is following us looking for a feed," I replied.

"Well, he's not getting me yet," said Steve, hurriedly getting himself back in the raft and securing the flaps.

I resumed my inspection of my legs, gingerly pulling up my jeans. Shit, it was noticeably worse than yesterday, the red welt running down my shin wider and redder than before. And the ulcer on my other leg was deeper and uglier. There were sores covering my whole body, not a square inch of my skin free of infection. I felt where the muscles of my thighs and calves had once been, and they were now all limp and flaccid. It was depressing. I pulled the legs of my jeans down and they came apart in my hands. I cursed as I tore off the rotting pieces of fabric, trying to save as much as I could. I needed the protection, the vital insulation that it provided me. Steve was sleeveless and his jeans had disintegrated below his knees, and I wondered how he coped with the cold.

My jumper was helping to keep me alive. Wool was the best insulation and its resistance to water was well known. The instructor at the Australian Maritime College came again to my mind. "Okay gentleman, it is survival night in the pool. Wear your normal sea gear, and don't forget your woollen jumper." By the end of the night there were only three of us left standing, or swimming, the rest having succumbed to the large heater fans at the side of the pool, desperately and miserably trying to get warm. They had not brought woollen jumpers as instructed. They had brought jumpers made from synthetic materials. So I had always worn a pure woollen jumper at sea, and this one had saved my life and was continuing to do so.

As I lay there thinking, I cast my eyes around the raft and it occurred to me that something was amiss. Apart from the two cotton rags, the whistle and the paddle, we had two lengths of rope, each a few metres long, and the remains of the heaving line – but one of the pieces was not in its place. It had been securely tied so it could not have washed away. And it had been there last night. There was only one place where it could be. A wry smile crossed my face. So we were both playing the same deadly game. I lay back down and curled up next to Steve, this time, and every time from then on, sleeping with my fist clenched and tucked firmly under my chin to protect my throat from a garrotte.

As I lay there, my thoughts turned to my children. I remembered another tight spot I had been in early in 1990 when I was taking a small timber vessel from Sydney to Western Samoa to make my fortune in the South Pacific, catching yellowfin and big-eye tuna. There were two of us on that voyage, myself as well as my younger brother Andrew. Halfway between New Caledonia and Fiji we were swept into the eye of a category five cyclone, Cyclone Fran. With winds of over one hundred knots and mountainous seas over a hundred feet high, we were battling for our lives. The autopilot had been smashed and we were down to hand steering. We had had no food or sleep for over two days and were desperately tired. At the end of a short watch I looked down at Andrew, his life jacket on, sleeping on the wheelhouse floor with water rushing all around him. He looked peaceful and I wanted to just lie down there with him. The storm had beaten me, there was no way we were going to survive the mountainous seas. My boat, *Marango Bay,* was literally falling apart. I looked up and saw Sophie – Daniel had not been born at the time – standing on the deck, watching me through the wheelhouse windows, dressed in her best Sunday dress and clutching her ruggy. She smiled her precious smile and said in a clear voice over the screaming of the wind, "Daddy, come home."

She had seemed so real standing there that I felt as though I could have gone out and grabbed her. I stood transfixed, blinked my eyes a few times, and then Sophie had vanished as quickly as she had appeared. Clearly, I had been hallucinating. I gritted my teeth, determined to go on, and the next few waves did not seem to be as enormous as before. From that moment on we slowly crawled our way out of the path of the storm to safety and I firmly believe that Sophie had saved me. Just when I was about to give up, she had come and called me safely home and her words were echoing in my head as our ninth day on the raft ended. Daddy's coming home, I promised, as I lay there with tears in my eyes.

Day 10
Preparing to Die

If I were to survive this ordeal, there were three more days to go until I achieved my second goal of reaching Vietnam in thirteen days. Could I do it, I lay there wondering. We had had no food in ten days, precious little water, were in a disintegrating, leaky raft and now had a killer stalking us. I was getting weaker and weaker but knew that I had to keep trying, that I must never give up. Every day gave us a fresh chance of rescue. So I had to survive the night.

Maybe I would get to eat Steve tomorrow but I needed him to live through tonight. Without one another we would freeze to death, and if we were capsized or swamped, one person wouldn't be able to right the raft on their own. We had had a good day, with very little water entering the raft. The little that had sprayed in was gathered in a small pool under the double bottom and it could stay there. It wasn't worth the energy needed to remove it. We shuffled into our night positions, me driving, Steve cuddled up by my side. The night settled in and it had started to get cold. "I hate the night," I murmured.

There was a muffled reply, "Hate the nights."

The rushing sound of a breaking wave approached rapidly. I leant back and raised my legs, pulling harder on the reins. The wave smashed into us and passed safely under, hardly a drop getting into the raft. Come on give us your best, I goaded the weather. Blow, you bastard, blow. Blow us to Vietnam.

I could not stay in my position for as long as I had on previous nights, but I forced myself to stay until I could take it no more. Cold, stiff and exhausted, I nudged Steve. "Could you take over for a while, mate? I'm fucked."

"No worries," he replied.

We did our drunken life raft shuffle and managed to change positions. I was cold and shivering, and cuddled up next to Steve and fell into an exhausted sleep. It didn't seem as though I had been asleep for long when Steve nudged me awake. "Want to take over for a spell? I can't lie like this much longer."

"No worries," I replied. And we did our drunken dance and settled ourselves again.

The raft carried us through the night, but our ability to stay on watch was growing shorter and shorter. During the night on one of Steve's watches we took another scary ride, surfing on the back of a large breaker. "I thought we were gone there, mate," said Steve shakily.

I let out my breath. My heart was thumping wildly, pumped by adrenalin and fear. "Wild ride mate, bloody wild ride," I said.

We calmed ourselves and changed positions again. I took the reins and occupied my mind by doing my sums. At nearly ten days at sixty miles a day we must have covered six hundred nautical miles by now. If I was right, there were only a couple of hundred miles to go. I can't die now, I can't give up, I kept telling myself; we were getting closer all the time. I thought about the dirty water and the confused sea a few days ago, and the birds and the flotsam. We must have swept close by Hainan Island. Clouds slowed as they approached a large landmass, building and increasing in strength as the heat of the land slowed them, and then they started to dump their rain. This was consistent with the few mouthfuls of rain that we had managed to collect; lighter rain as we approached land, the big downpours as we passed it and then a tapering off as we drifted away. We must be well past Hainan by now, as that was days ago. I have to get through the night, I repeated to myself, over and over again.

I shuddered as I thought of the night. Everything bad happens at night; everything bad. I thought about the risks if we made landfall at night. I had discounted any hope of a white sandy beach; I was convinced we would have to contend with cliffs and rocks, and reefs and coral. In this sea of well over four metres, these would form a deadly barrier.

We would have little or no warning before we slammed into them in the dark and I shuddered at the thought of the terror and horror that would follow. A shiver of fear consumed me and I closed my eyes, shaking my head from side to side. No, no, no, how many more obstacles, how many more tests of will, of strength, would we have to endure? The night; just get through the night. We might be rescued tomorrow, I said to myself; forget about the rest, deal with that if and when we have to.

I hung on to the reins of the raft for as long as I possibly could, my body screaming in agony. I was losing track of why I was here. What heinous crime had I committed to be subjected to such extreme torture? Why me? Whatever the reason, I *was* here, my body disintegrating before my eyes. I was dying of exposure, dehydration and starvation, if a shark or drowning didn't get me first. My mind and body had had enough. I nudged Steve. "Could you take it for a while mate, I've had it."

"Yeah mate, give me a sec to get organised," he replied groggily. I collapsed next to Steve and went straight back to hell: the tormentors, the judges, and the accusers. I was now living a nightmare, the horrors of which knew no boundaries. As I slowly regained consciousness, renewed disbelief took over, and then shock and numbness as the reality of our situation dawned on me for the tenth new day. Could it get any worse? I lay there trying to breathe; my eyes were watering, and my nose burning. My skin felt like it was burning. I smelt the neck of my jumper. Disgusting man, I said to myself, grimacing. I smelt the double bottom. Damn, that was just as bad and the air inside the raft was stifling. I was lying in and soaked in a mixture of thick brown urine and sea water and the ammonia was actually overcoming me. I couldn't take it any longer, I had to get up. I struggled to my knees and fumbled with the lashings at the opening and flung open the flaps. A blast of fresh air hit me in the face and I sat there sucking it in, looking out at the ocean. The clouds had lifted and there was no sign of rain. As always, of course, we were completely alone.

I thought of Kurt and my family. Surely they must realise we were missing by now. What were they doing? What were they thinking? Were they organising a search? Did they even know where to start? How could they possibly guess where the boat went down or that we were now over six hundred miles from that position? It was clear that no one was going to find us; we were completely on our own.

Steve had also stirred, also overcome by the cloying fumes of the urine. "Fuck me, I feel like shit," he said. "Me too, we've got to do something about this piss before it kills me." My skin was burning, stinging and itching as the foul brew ate into it, its access made easy through the thousands of weeping sores covering my body. We tried mopping and sponging out the mess but it was no good. It had impregnated the rubber, soaked into our skin, our clothes, and our hair. "There's only one thing for it, we have to flood the raft. It's the only way," I said.

It went against everything we had endured over the past week or so, to actually put water into the raft on purpose. All we had been doing for the past nine and a half days was completely at odds with this, driving ourselves unmercifully to clear the water out and keep the raft from being swamped. I looked at my small rag and clenched my red raw fist, grimacing at the task ahead. "We have got to rinse our bodies and clothes as well," I told Steve.

"I was going to do that anyway. My skin feels like shit," he replied.

We sat for ages, the canopy pulled down around our waists, scanning the ocean all around for the shark. "See him?" I asked Steve after some time.

"Nup. Nothing," he replied.

"Okay, let's get this over and done with," I said. Firmly grasping the grab rope I slid over the side, followed quickly by Steve. The water actually felt good; it was cool and refreshing. I ducked my head under, using my free hand to wash the water over my hair and face. I also opened my eyes to clear the piss from my stinging pupils and to look around. I spun quickly, but there was nothing but a ghostly blue haze. Surfacing, I got my chest up onto the side of the raft alongside Steve and pushed down. A torrent of water poured in over the side. We tipped ourselves forward with the surging water and slipped safely back inside.

"That fucker can stay hungry," I gasped to Steve, adrenalin pumping through me, my heart racing with the realisation that I had knowingly and willingly jumped into the sea with a hungry shark. I have seen plenty of mako jaws, prehistoric harbingers of death, and the thought of them crunching down into my body was a bit much to contemplate.

I collapsed against the raft, recovering from the shock of this realisation, the sea water covering my legs.

"We had better make a start," I said a few minutes later. Every movement sapped my strength. Balancing on my cramped knees, grasping the side of the raft for support, I bent over with my eyes closed and began. Sophie, Daniel, Sophie, Daniel, Sophie, Daniel – it went on forever, trickle after trickle wrung from my rag. Our pace was a lot slower now, but we still matched ourselves one for one, never faltering until the job was done.

"I'll have a rest while I put some air into the raft," said Steve after a while.

I knelt there exhausted, doubting that I would be able to find the strength or energy to do it. Thank God it was not my turn. A few minutes later Steve lowered himself to the valve and started blowing. The effort told on him, but when he raised himself, red faced and breathing hard, the raft was firm again. "Good one mate, that feels better," I said to him.

The raft was dry and inflated again, the stench of urine gone, and the last thing to do before collapsing was to have a look around. I scanned the horizon, letting out a sigh of despair and desolation. There was nothing; just the sea, the clouds and us. I ducked my head back inside and closed the flaps, and fell onto my back alongside Steve, my eyes watching the inside of the raft buckling and twisting under the hammering blows of the waves. I wondered how long it could possibly take this punishment. One tortured air ring was the only thing keeping us alive.

Again I closed my eyes in torment, unable to control my thoughts. What would go first, the raft or us? There was no point thinking about it, it was purely academic. I just wanted to rest, to forget about everything, but my mind was in total confusion, short-circuiting, losing control. I heard Steve mutter something.

"I didn't hear," I said.

He spoke louder, "I am going to pray to God."

I kept lying there, staring at the roof of the canopy. This is what it had come to. Even though I could not register defeat, the realisation dawned on me that I had to prepare to die. I knew I must pray as well. I had been introduced to God as a child, when I went regularly to church with my parents. It had been a long time between drinks but I took a deep breath and started.

"Dear God, I know you are a very busy man. I wouldn't blame you if you didn't even hear me, an invisible speck on the ocean, unworthy of your time. Your problems are huge; you have millions of starving children, millions of starving people to care for. You have millions of people dying from terrible diseases, disastrous wars and natural disasters. You are witnessing your creation destroying your beautiful planet. I understand how busy you are, but I want to tell you all the bad things I have done." I turned my memory back, right back as far as I could go to my early childhood. There was no point in lying to God. I couldn't leave anything out. I methodically listed all my sins in my mind: the relentless teasing of my siblings, the squabbles, the fights; the disappointments, the angst I had caused my parents; the stupid things I had done at school, upsetting my friends and hurting my lovers. The list went on and on, every sin. It flowed out easily. Nobody else could hear, only God. And then it was done. "Dear God, these are all the bad and wrong things I have done, I am very sorry I did any of them. I just want to ask if you will please forgive me. I know you can't pluck me out of the sea, but can you show me how to get the strength to live? Thank you for listening to me. I hope you heard, but I wouldn't blame you if you didn't; how could you possibly know I was here?"

I felt better when I had done this, as though a burden had been lifted from me. I actually felt at peace with myself and drifted off to sleep, and this time I didn't go to hell. This time I visited my family and friends. I had begun to hallucinate and was out of my body, sitting propped up in the raft, which was in the corner of a lounge room filled with my family and friends. It seemed all very normal – good conversation, kind people, a seemingly everyday experience. Everyone was glad to see me, but they had a faraway, sad look in their eyes. I couldn't figure out why I wasn't offered, nor why I didn't ask for, any drink or food. My guests were tucking into cakes and biscuits and sipping all manner of drinks, but offered none to me. The other odd thing was that I couldn't get out of the raft and nobody offered to help me. But none of that really mattered because I was happy to see everyone again.

A breaking sea roared past and missed the raft by inches. I flinched and stirred. Dumbfounded, I looked around the lounge room as I was shaken back to reality. Oh God, I *was* back to reality, there was no escape. I was back in the raft in the middle of the sea. I had to get up to clear my brain. As I worked on the lashing I noticed that my fingers looked like white and red sticks, nails shattered, loose skin draped over the bones. I cursed, half at the sight of my hands and half at the stiff and unyielding knots. I pulled back the flaps and took a deep breath and the fresh air brought me fully awake. I searched the ocean carefully but there was still nothing in sight. My mind raced back to the flares, the radio, the torch, the EPIRB. None of this should have happened, I wailed to myself. I slammed my fist into the raft in frustration. I had spent ten days in this storm, with no food and hardly any water, battling to survive. I estimated that we had three more days before we would reach Vietnam. Could I really hope to survive another three days? I scanned the sky behind us. The clouds were higher with not a hint of rain in sight. I sat there pondering my fate, shaking my head in disbelief.

After a bit I took my piece of rag and began absentmindedly mopping out some of the spray that had come aboard during the day. Steve got up and helped. When we had finished and had closed up the canopy I decided to have another look at my legs; they were beginning to get very sore. I pulled up my jeans, or what was left of them. "Oh fuck me!" I cried aloud.

Steve looked at my legs and grimaced. "Shit mate, that doesn't look good."

"You're not wrong there man," I answered. The red sore running down my shin had doubled in size, its centre a dark cherry red, nearly black, with angry and swollen red tendrils spreading around my calf. I gingerly probed the black area running down my shinbone. Oh my God, it *was* my shinbone; I could not feel any skin! The constant grinding of my wet shins into the denim and rubber had worn the skin off my shinbone. Now my leg was infected and the infection was worsening. The word 'gangrene' leapt into my mind. This must be the beginning of the end. I couldn't fight the infection, and gangrene would set in and I would die in agony. I checked the rest of my body, which was deteriorating at an alarming rate. I lay back down, full of sadness, loneliness and despair. How could I give up now, when we were so close, I asked myself? I didn't want to die. So again, I made up my mind that I would make it through the night; I had to, because tomorrow we might be saved, and then there would have been no point dying in the middle of the night. No point at all.

Day 11
Final Barriers

As the night enveloped us again we stumbled and tumbled into our positions, our movements slow and painful. My legs and ankles resting on the lower ring hurt and both my Achilles tendons were rubbed raw. I pushed my shoulders into the far side of the ring. "Okay mate," I said to Steve. He cuddled up next to me, his bare arm inside my jumper. Normally warm and comforting, now it felt cold and clammy against my stomach. "I hate the nights," I mumbled.

"I hate the nights," came the reply.

Before long I was freezing cold and shaking and I felt I couldn't take much more. As a deafening roar approached, I used what little energy I had left to pull back and lift my legs, but nothing happened and the breaking wave smashed into us, with gallons of water jetting inside. I had no strength left, and I realised with dismay that my legs hadn't actually raised up and my arms hadn't pulled. For the first time in more than ten days, we didn't get up and bail the water out. It was squashing out from under the double bottom from our weight and we were lying in small pools of water. I shouted at the wind, "Blow you bastard, blow!" The raft bucked and swayed and my Achilles tendons chafed. My body was numb and I felt that I simply couldn't go on. I called to Steve, "I am really fucked man. I can't lie here like this any longer."

"No worries, little buddy; I'll swap with you," he replied. With enormous effort we laboriously changed positions. I pulled my sodden jumper over my ears, the foil hood and sock having long ago disintegrated and succumbed to the sea, and pushed my face into Steve's side. My shoulders, hips and legs were resting in pools of cold water and I no longer cared. I was beyond exhaustion. I hate the nights, I repeated to myself. Everything bad happened at night.

This proved to be correct yet again, as the nightmares began. I plunged straight back into hell with crying children, photos on the mantelpiece, bloated bodies, the accusers and the judges. Even the crashing waves were only momentary distractions as I became submerged in my nightmares. My mind and body were being tortured beyond their limits, my soul deprived of comfort. There was no escape, no stopping the onslaught.

I woke in the middle of the night curled up in a ball, freezing cold, my body immersed in water. I felt for Steve in the darkness; he had slipped from his position through sheer exhaustion and was lying curled up on the other side of the raft. My mind screamed at me to get up, get up! Get the water out! If you sleep in the water you will die. But my body would not respond; could not respond. It didn't want to move. I managed with enormous effort to lean over and nudge Steve who awoke, shivering violently. "We've got to get the water out of her mate or we won't survive the night. We'll be dead by the morning."

Running on sheer willpower we started the job. Thankfully there wasn't a lot of water, just enough to kill us. I rocked back and forth like I had for the past ten days. Sophie, Daniel, Sophie, Daniel, I wailed within. Would I ever see them again? I cried but there were no tears. No tears? I really was running on empty, the precious liquid already consumed by my ravenous body. Hours later, after securing the canopy, we collapsed on the bottom of the raft. "I can't sit up there any more, mate," I said to Steve.

"Neither can I, it's too much, too cold."

"Let's just lie like we used to and hope nothing happens," I said. We cuddled up as close and as tight as we could and began to feel a bit better, a far cry from lying cuddled up freezing to death in a pool of cold water. We lay there, unmoving, each in our private hell, as the sea and the wind pushed us through the cold blackness. The water sprayed and jetted in but we were impervious to it by then. The water slowly pooled underneath us again. It was a terrible night. I have no words to describe it. It was hell on earth. I had no strength left and the nightmares continued unabated. Mercifully, the sky finally began to lighten and the dawning day brought some warmth into the raft. In my confused and damaged state of mind I knew only one thing: I wasn't going to give up, but neither could I make it through another night. I knew my body was about finished; it was nothing but red-raw skin and bones.

My mind screamed at me to get the water out of the raft but nothing happened. I couldn't move. Maybe later, I thought as I closed my eyes. I was too tired to do it now. And then the hallucinations and out-of-body experiences returned in earnest. I sat happily with my children, family and friends. It seemed so real, so nice, and so peaceful. As I moved in and out of consciousness, I realised that my body was shutting down and it occurred to me that this was a nice, peaceful way to go. My brain had dispensed with the torture, and was now comforting me as the end drew closer.

Another wave splashed inside and the water was getting too much again. I couldn't lie there anymore. I had to get the water out. Somehow, I managed to struggle to my knees and my movements woke Steve, who also battled to get upright. Together we untied the canopy and looked outside and as always, the same sight greeted us – an empty, endless rolling ocean.

"Things are a bit grim, Skip," Steve said, as he stared out at the sea.

"Yeah mate, things are getting grim alright. I don't know how I got through the night; I don't know how much longer I can go on really. I'm just about fucked," I replied.

"Same here, mate. I've just about had it too."

We started mopping with our pitiful pieces of rag and managed to get the bulk of the water out, but that was all we could manage. I slumped next to the opening, recovering my breath. The clouds looked a bit darker and lower. Maybe we would get some rain today. We'd had no water for two days now, and I was desperately thirsty. I closed the canopy and collapsed into the double bottom.

Self-pity forced its way into my consciousness. Why me? What had I done to deserve this? Why should I die? I didn't have an incurable disease, there was nothing wrong with me, I wasn't ready to die, damn, I didn't want to die. Sadness, frustration and grief flooded through me, my despair indescribable. I floated back to the comfort of my family and watched them eating and drinking. But they still wouldn't help me out of the raft. Somebody said, "Look, it's raining," and pointed out the window. I was startled back to reality. It *was* raining; a steady beat on the canopy.

"It's raining, it's raining!" I cried to Steve. The desire to drink overcame our weakened bodies and we struggled to get our arms and heads outside. We both got two small mouthfuls before it stopped and I savoured every drop. It was the tiniest recharge, but I looked around and there was more rain on the horizon, draped under low, black clouds. "Let's not give up hope, there's more rain coming, mate. We'll get another drink today," I said to Steve, as we closed up the canopy.

My thoughts drifted off to my children. If I never saw them again, didn't get the chance to say goodbye, they would spend their lives not knowing what happened to me. As

I dropped into unconsciousness my last thoughts were of Sophie. "Daddy, come home." She had saved me from that other storm.

I sank into a deep, deep sleep and then Steve was pushing me. "Rain! Rain! It's raining! Wake up!" he was shouting, already working frantically at the canopy. I clenched my eyes as I clawed my way back to consciousness. The nightmares seemed so real and yet I was in the here and now as well. Somehow I got to my knees and pushed my head outside as the rain abruptly stopped. "Fuck me!" cried Steve, and collapsed back inside.

I sat by the side to recover from the ordeal of moving. I scanned the clouds for more rain. There was a massive dark cloud low over the water a few miles away. It must be bucketing down over there, but it was going to miss us completely. And then I took another look because something didn't seem quite right; it was too dark, too low. Adrenalin and disbelief coursed through me as I checked again; it was land, it was a bloody island, and we had just gone past it.

"Land! Land! An island!" I shouted to Steve. I couldn't believe what I was seeing; it was a low island, flat topped and densely vegetated, about a mile long. It was land but we had missed it. I tore the canopy down and looked in the direction we were heading in. Oh my God, another island, right in front of us, this one much larger, with two weathered peaks of extinct volcanoes! It was five or six miles long and we looked to be heading straight for the middle of it. Steve and I just stared at this apparition in awe, our hearts thumping. We were about two miles from the island, possibly an hour away. Was this our salvation? The excitement and adrenalin was pumping through me. I studied the angles of our approach again, the peaks of the volcano, the other island. It was clear that we were being funnelled by the wind and current towards the gap between the two islands.

I made my decision: it was all or nothing. I could not survive another night. "We have to make that island, we have to paddle across the wind or we will drift past it," I said to Steve.

He was of the exact same mind. "We have to make the island, buddy. Let's get to it."

We laid on the collapsed canopy and started paddling. Steve used the oar and I my hands. Pull, pull, we urged ourselves. But we seemed to be getting nowhere, our angle of approach changing all the time. Soon we were lined up on the northern point of the island but clearly we were going to drift past it. I could now see buildings and towers rising above the foliage. "Oh my God, it's inhabited! There are people on the island. Oh dear God, we're going to miss it!" I looked closely at the end of the island and my hopes leapt anew; there was something there, a spit of sand. I could see palm trees or light poles along its length. My heart was pounding in my chest; maybe we were going to be alright.

The next we knew, we were heading straight towards a sandy beach. We paddled frantically, urging ourselves onward. The island was growing in size; the buildings had become clearly visible. Suddenly, I stopped paddling, fear gripping me again. It wasn't a white sandy beach at all, it was a reef.

The white line I had mistaken for sand was a line of massive breakers, crashing onto coral. The light poles, clearly visible by now, were masts of vessels anchored in the lee of the reef, protected from the storm. Oh dear God, we were now headed for the centre of the reef, powerless to stop or change our course. "It's a fucking reef, Steve," I muttered. We both stopped paddling and contemplated our fate. The line of massive breaking waves was approaching fast.

"What can we do?" asked Steve.

"Nothing much at all mate, but I'm staying here. No way am I getting back into the raft."

"Same here," he replied. We could plainly see the anchored vessels now. Maybe, just maybe, if we survived the reef we could get to one of them, I thought desperately. The reef was getting closer, a sound like thunder filling our ears. There was no time to think, there was no time to prepare. We entered the line of breakers, the swells rearing above us, twice their normal height. I slipped over the side of the raft and hung on as Steve did the same. I noticed he threaded his arm around and around the grab ropes but I couldn't do it, the fear of being hopelessly tangled in the raft not appealing to me at all. "Good luck, mate!" I shouted to Steve.

"Good luck to you too, little buddy!" he called back.

I looked up straight into the face of a huge breaking wave. It broke right on top of us with an indescribable force. I was torn from the raft and pushed under, cartwheeling and spinning in a frenzy of churning, thundering water. This is it, I thought, this is how it ends. I struggled to the surface, choking and gasping, as another wall of white water came rushing at me, only metres away. I only had time to suck in half a breath before I ducked under. A crazy thought went through my mind: this was just what I used to do when I was a kid, playing in the surf at Long Beach at Robe, an idyllic fishing and holiday village on the south-east coast of South Australia. That was where I had first taken to the sea, sailing my mirror dinghy as far as I dared across the bay.

Under and down I went, spinning in the churning cauldron, my stretched jumper twisting all around, hampering my movements. I tried to take it off but I couldn't, it was too twisted up. I arrived back at the surface, retching and gagging in the welter of bubbles and foam. There was no time for anything; another half breath and I was forced under again. I kicked the remains of my jeans off to free my legs as I spun wildly in the confusion. This had to be the end – but somehow I made my way back to the surface. I glimpsed the island and then another wall of white water came at me, as I gulped another breath and was forced under again. I was getting really tired; what small amount of strength I had left was fast running out. My breath had gone and I opened the corner of my mouth and let the sea water trickle in. I knew that all it would take would be just one breath and I would finally be at peace. But I could hear Sophie and Daniel screaming at me from the recesses of my brain, "Daddy, come home!"

I blindly lashed out for the surface and a few agonising seconds later, my head broke through. I gasped and choked as I tried to suck air into my lungs, but another wave hit me and pushed me forward. This time I wasn't forced under, but I was still fighting for air in the turbulent water. I was spent and couldn't keep myself up any more, and my feet drifted down and touched bottom. With what little strength I had left I pushed up, as it dawned on me that my waist was actually clear of the water. I couldn't believe it; I was standing on the fucking reef, on land, sort of. There was something solid under my feet.

I spun around and looked back. How on earth had I got through that, I wondered, as I gazed at the towering lines of breaking waves. Turning my back on them I searched in the direction of the island, which was still a good half a mile away. The raft? Steve? Where were they? I spotted the raft with Steve clinging to it, holding it against the wind and current on the far side of the reef, a hundred metres or more away. I shouted and screamed as I started to wade towards him. "Steve! Steve! Stay there, stay there! I'm coming, stay there Steve!" I don't know where I found the strength but suddenly I was like an Olympic athlete, charging through the water. Nothing was going to stop me now. I staggered and fell on the coral, and stumbled into holes that took me out of my depth. But I kept going, never stopping and shouting all the way, "Steve, stay there, I'm coming!"

Cuts, bruises, stingrays, spikes or urchins – none of them mattered. I had to get back onto the raft or I would be dead. I kept calling out to Steve and by the time I neared the raft I was sobbing, "Please stay, Steve. Steve!" and took one last lurch. I grasped the side of the raft, panting with exhaustion, the adrenalin draining away in spasms.

"Never thought I'd see you again," Steve said.

"Thought I was fucked there, mate," I choked out.

"You were in the surf a long time, then I saw your ugly little head pop out on the reef. Fuck me." He explained what had happened to him. "Simple, I just hung on. It was one wild ride, and this is where I ended up. I've been looking for you ever since. Shit man, what do we do now?"

"We have to get to the island," I said. "Let's drag the raft over the reef and see if we can get closer." The island was in front of us half a mile away. The wind and current were pushing us sideways as we struggled towards it. Before we had covered twenty paces we fell off the edge of the reef into deep water. The wind and current grabbed hold of us and were going to drift us past the island. "Paddle Steve, we've got to paddle!" Lying on top of the canopy we started madly thrashing the water with our hands. The raft was soft and loose after the terrible beating the surf had just given it. It was just about finished. We had to make it to the island or even to one of the boats, I thought in desperation. I kept paddling with my hands, urging the broken raft on, but when I next looked up, I could see we weren't going to make it, not even to one of the boats. The wind and current were too strong. It was too much to bear. My mind was reeling. Everything had happened too fast. I kept paddling, harder and harder. When I looked up again, I saw a small boat on a cresting wave, stick-like figures in it silhouetted against the evening sky before it disappeared down the back of a wave.

"A boat, Steve! A boat! I saw a boat! Over there, close to the point!" I cried, pointing. And then we could both see it, but it seemed to be heading away, towards the anchored vessels. We started waving and shouting but it continued on its course. We were transfixed – shouting, screaming, and waving. Please, dear God, let them see us! The boat appeared and disappeared several times and by then was almost past us. When it was directly down wind of us it suddenly veered around and pushed into the sea and headed directly for us. At first I refused to believe it, and kept yelling and screaming and waving, with Steve doing the same. But the boat kept coming towards us, and we could see men gathering at the bow, waving back to us.

Other human beings! Waving to us! We had been seen! Exhilaration and a torrent of other emotions swept through me. We were saved! We laughed and slapped our hands together. "We made it! We made it!" we chorused. And then there it was alongside us, a small fishing vessel with high pointed bows. But it didn't look so small to us. From where we sat on the raft it towered above us. I tried to reach up, but I couldn't. My body would not respond and I fell into the water. I felt hands grabbing me and strong arms lifted me clear and I was dragged over the board and lowered gently onto the deck. My body couldn't move. I could only lie staring at the deck. I noticed it was dry and sun bleached and the heads of loose nails were sticking out in places. We had been saved. Our ordeal was over.

Or so we thought.

Ly Son Island

I tried to sit up but I couldn't. All I could do was raise my head above the bulwark of the boat. I looked around and counted seven men. Steve was sitting in the middle of the boat and the remains of the raft were draped over the stern. What looked like the eldest of the crew was squatting beside me, his hand on my head, talking softly and gently. I couldn't understand a word that he was saying. Everything was unreal and I couldn't grasp what was happening. I was just a witness, watching what was happening and what would happen next.

As we drew close to the island, I could see people lined up along a low stone sea wall; not dozens or hundreds of people, but thousands of them. It had started to rain and the wind was still close to gale force, and the people were being drenched by the rain and spray from the sea as it broke against the stone wall. Our boat was headed straight for the crowd. A dozen or more similar craft to ours were moored close by. The coxswain manoeuvred the boat through the maze of long mooring lines stretching out over the shallow coral bottom and we were soon secured. There was lots of shouting backwards and forwards and all I could do was wonder why they wouldn't take us ashore.

Eventually there was a commotion at the steps of the sea wall and the crowd parted, and I could see a man lowering a wicker basket about two metres round into the water. First wading, then swimming, he pushed it out to our boat. Four plastic bags were passed up from the basket, two for me and two for Steve. They each contained a brand new pair of shorts and a lightweight synthetic soccer top and I was urged to put them on. Apart from the remains of my woollen jumper I was naked, but I wasn't able to get into the clothes. My body had shut down; the exertion of getting over the reef had been the last straw. The man, who had never left my side since I had been pulled onto the boat, gently dressed me. Then someone picked me up and lowered me into the wicker basket. Curled up in the foetal position, I was pushed ashore, where more strong hands carried me up the steps, the crowd parting like the Red Sea as I was moved to a low canvas tent close by. There I was placed on the ground next to a small charcoal fire, Steve joining me a few minutes later. The crowd pressed around us, the first row sitting, the next kneeling, the next squatting and the rest standing. They formed a solid mass around us, a human wall against the elements. They were all silently staring at us as if we were aliens.

A woman came to my side and squeezed a small amount of fluid from a drink box into a cup and handed it to me. I was being handed a drink! Was this really happening or was it another cruel nightmare? I took the cup and swallowed the fluid. It was sweet and fruit flavoured and I felt intoxicated by the pleasure of its taste and feel – it was unbelievable. It was Steve's turn next. "Man, that felt good," I said to him.

"Unreal," he said, sipping at the drink.

There was a bit of shuffling in the crowd and two small bowls appeared. The same woman handed one to each of us along with a china spoon; it was a broth of warm rice. I dipped my spoon in and with shaking hands took my first small mouthful of food in more than eleven days. Whatever had been added to the rice I didn't know, but it tasted fantastic. I could not believe that I was actually eating. I was offered another small drink and my trembling hands clutched the cup as I swallowed the contents. Oh man, was I ever hungry and thirsty. I needed more, I wanted more. I held my empty bowl up to the woman and pleaded for more. She shook her head, sadness and concern on her face. I begged for more. "Please . . . *please*," I begged. She shook her head again and there were tears in her eyes.

At that point the crowd around us surged and there were uniforms everywhere; caps, badges, shouts and commands. Before I knew it I was lifted from the floor of the tent and carried through the press of people. The crowd opened a path for us and I was placed on a small motorbike behind the driver. My feet were placed on the pegs and another man squeezed on behind me, wrapping his arms around me and the driver, effectively locking me in. I rested the side of my head against the driver's back and we started to move, winding our way through the gathering crowd. The motorbikes cleared the throng and picked up speed. I felt like I was watching the world flash past from a window in a train. Small houses, huts, open-shuttered shops, sheds and fences passed by. People were alerted by the cavalcade of bikes sounding their horns continuously to clear a path, and stopped what they were doing to stare at us as we went by.

Where was I and who were these people? The bike was undulating on the road; no, it was the road that was rocking. I searched for a reason why. It had to be a floating island; I could remember reading about them. Islands of reeds, this had to be one of those, the rocking movement caused by the sea as it passed underneath. I was in another world. I didn't really know what was going on. The houses, shops, huts and staring people kept flashing past and it was dark by the time we pulled off the road and stopped next to a white, double-storey building which I vaguely registered to be a hospital. By the time I had been carried up the short flight of stairs at the entrance to the building, thirty or forty motorbikes were in the courtyard and people were coming from all directions to form another huge crowd. I was carried in and placed on a bed in a large room on the ground floor. Steve was carried in and placed on another bed. There were people everywhere; a sea of white jackets and dresses, green uniforms, brown uniforms, and suits mixed with other colours of the crowd. The people in white closed in and started searching, probing and listening to my body. They spoke to me but I couldn't understand a word. I kept repeating that I spoke English, English only.

A woman sat down on the bed next to me and put her hand gently on my head. I looked up and recognised her as the woman in the tent. She unwrapped a silk scarf revealing another drink box and it tasted just as delicious as before, but she would only let me have a few sips before taking the container away again. I begged for more but she refused, indicating with her hands that I must slow down and take it slowly. I looked around and could see that the crowd was being herded out of the room by the uniforms. They gathered outside, their faces and hands pressed to the curtainless windows, staring at us in silence. But the woman refused to budge and after a quick conversation between her and one of the uniforms, she remained at my side.

Then the uniforms started on me. They were all asking questions, and were right in my face. I couldn't understand a word and just kept repeating, "English, English." Two new people were ushered into the room, a man and a woman and the man came over to me. After consulting with the group of uniforms that had gathered at my bed, he looked at me and in barely coherent English said, "I am going to ask you some questions, do you understand?"

I nodded my head, but got the first question in. "Where am I?" I asked.

"Vietnam," said the man.

And then the interrogation started. Who, where, what? They were confused; an Australian and a New Zealander with no passports or documents, no proof of identity. Where had we dropped our crew, why were there only two of us, where were our crew? They thrust pieces of paper into my hand and told me to write down addresses, phone numbers, names, and places. These were snatched away and more paper was given to me. Write it all down again, the process went on. The uniforms then turned their attention to Steve. I heard the same questions, the same demands. The woman gave me another beautiful sip of that precious liquid. I glanced around the room and at the faces pressed against the windows. There was another patient, a baby being cradled by her mother, on the other side of the room, the baby squealing in pain as the mother positioned her over a nappy. I watched as a stream of brown fluid spurted out on it. Poor little thing, I remember thinking, I hope she gets better soon.

The uniforms came back with interpreters and the entire process was repeated. There was more writing on little pieces of paper; maps, numbers and names. I was starting to get tired of it all. One of the uniforms kept getting up close and shouting three words at me over and over again. "Where you from? Where you from?" "Australia, mate, I've told you a hundred fucking times," I kept replying.

A conversation took place between the people in white and the uniforms. An interpreter explained that the questions had finished for now but that there would be more again tomorrow. Steve and I were being moved. We were placed on stretchers and carried upstairs to a small room where there were two beds, a cupboard, a small table and a chair, and a large double window facing out to the front of the hospital. The walls along the corridor were glass from waist height up and the door also. Doctors came in and gave us both another check over and nurses arrived carrying all sorts of trays and tins. Roll over, jab. Three or four different tablets were placed in my hands along with a small cup of water and swallowing motions were made. They studied my infected legs, probing them with their gloved fingers. The nurse washed and cleaned the wounds on my legs, and the same woman from before came in and sat next to my bed, smiling at me and chatting away with the hospital staff. Again she produced the drink box and gave me a sip. I read the label and it was in English on one side. Orange flavoured soy; it tasted delicious. I pointed at the orange on the box. "Orange, orange," I said. I made the motions of peeling an orange and eating it. The woman nodded her head, indicating that she understood, and said something that I didn't understand.

Finally, Steve and I were as cleaned up as we were going to get. I was given another jab by the doctor who was pointing at my leg. By now my legs, arms and hands were covered in gauze bandages, with a thick cream holding these in place.

Two young guards entered the room and I recognised one of them as the one who had been shouting 'where you from?' in my face. This guard had one red star on his uniform and the other guard had none. I dubbed them guard number one and guard number two! The hospital staff cleaned everything away and left. The two young uniforms had a bit of a chat, perhaps more of an argument, with my newfound friend. I could tell that she was being made to leave the room.

I smelt food as soon as the door opened; it was a small bowl of the same rice broth, flavoured with garlic and what looked like chives. It was only a small portion and I savoured every last morsel. We were also given a cup of warm, weak tea of some description and sachets of chalky-tasting paste to swallow. The bowls and cups were cleared away.

Our two guards had set up camp in the opposite room, and I could see them through the doors across the corridor, unrolling their sleeping bags. One of them got into his bag, while the other came into our room, pulled the curtains tightly closed on the window before sitting down in the chair next to the door. While closing the curtains he couldn't help himself; he peered down at me and shouted, "Where you from?" but this time managed to expand on his vocabulary by also asking, "What your name?" I ignored him.

I looked around the room, which was moving, just like when I was on the road. I figured that the hospital must have been built of foam and paper or else it would surely have tumbled down. I marvelled at the moving foam and paper architecture. The wind was howling through the trees and the building's shutters slammed and the roof banged. The power had been switched off. I really still could not believe it, that I was lying on a bed and was dry and covered with a blanket. Had I really been saved? I closed my eyes and listened to the wind as the storm intensified. I shuddered as I thought of what the night would have brought us on the collapsed raft.

I slept until the dawn cast its light through the curtains. The room was still moving, the walls still made of foam and paper. The other guard was in the room now and he drew the curtains back and pushed open the windows. The light flooded in and not long after, the doctor and his assistants arrived. Steve and I were both given another thorough going over; blood pressure, temperatures, listening to our chests, another injection followed by another, and then the pills. Then the nurses started removing my dressings and cleaning my wounds. This was an incredibly painful process. I suffered through it by keeping focused on what I knew was coming next – food and drink. In it came, the same as last night. Delicious! I loved every mouthful. Another cup of warm tea, and then more sachets of white paste to be washed down with a small cup of water. "That feels good," I said to Steve.

"Sure does mate," he replied.

We got our first visitors for the day. The same woman from the night before came into the room, followed by another man I recognised. He was the person who had plucked me out of the water and had been by my side on the boat. At a guess he was the boat's captain. Six more men and three or four women followed him in. After some animated gesturing at her wedding ring and pointing at one another, it became clear that the woman and the captain were married and the three youngest men were their sons. The captain then pointed to some older men in the room who were standing side by side with their wives, showing us their wedding rings. I soon caught on that these men were the rescue crew and we all started laughing and shaking hands. I couldn't thank them enough and was full of gratitude. We couldn't understand a word that we were saying to one another but our meaning was clear.

The captain's wife produced a small bag of oranges from her shawl with a huge smile and handed one each to Steve and I. Unreal. An orange! I peeled mine and popped a segment into my mouth and chewed down on it. What a sensation. I loved that orange! Soon more people crowded into the small room until it was full from wall to wall, with even more people pressing themselves against the glass in the door leading to the corridor, all trying to get a peek at us. They just stood there quietly talking, looking at us all the time. A guard eventually shooed them all out, but he had quite a job; everybody was reluctant to leave. The last to be pushed out of the door was the captain's wife, protesting as she left.

I was tired, so tired, and went straight back to sleep. I was woken by one of the guards. "Up, up!" he said. People were filing into the room: suits and uniforms, badges and caps. The same interpreter came to my side and explained that these men wanted to ask us more questions. It was exactly the same as the night before: the same questions, the same answers, the same writing on bits of paper. And then it was repeated all over again. Finally, the notes and papers were all shuffled and divided up, and the officers and suits marched out.

Both of the interpreters stayed. They introduced themselves as Tan and Ky and both were English teachers at the local school. They had been very serious and formal during the interrogations, but now they were smiling and happy. They told us that we were on Ly Son Island, which was part of Vietnam. The soldiers were border guards and the suits were various police and security personnel. Tan and Ky told us there would be more questions to answer the following day and they promised to come every day to visit us. They had to leave to prepare lessons for the next day and we thanked them as they left.

There were more rounds in the afternoon with different doctors and nurses, and we were put through the same routine checks. This was followed by more food and drink, exactly the same as before and once again I enjoyed every mouthful. I lay back on the bed and it suddenly occurred to me that we hadn't contacted anyone, that no one knew that we were alive or where we were. I motioned to the guard and holding my hand to the side of my face with little finger and thumb extended, said "Telephone, telephone; I need telephone." He understood and left the room.

Returning a few minutes later, he crossed his arms over his chest and said, "No telephone, no telephone."

I started to feel frustrated again. I had to contact my children; my family would be worried sick. I couldn't imagine how Sophie and Daniel were coping by then, with me missing for twelve days. I asked again for a phone, but got a sterner, louder reply that time. "No telephone, no telephone. No, no, no." There was nothing I could do. I was too exhausted and weak to get up and hunt one down for myself, and I really needed to sleep. The wind was still roaring over us, tearing at the roof and shutters. I fell asleep in my wobbly foam room. I stirred a few times during the night, as gusts of wind slammed the shutters. I was uncomfortable as my body was aching and sore all over. "I hate the nights," I muttered, and from across the small room came the reply,

"I hate the nights."

We were woken the following morning by the shout of "Up, up!" from one of the guards, as he drew back the curtains and opened the windows. I opened my eyes. The room was still swaying gently on its foundations of reeds and straw, and I was still convinced the hospital was made of foam. The same routine as the day before was repeated – the doctor and nurses, the probing, the injections and tablets, the removal of dead flesh from my legs with a pair of blunt tweezers, and the dressing and bandaging up. This routine was repeated twice a day every day of our stay in the hospital, followed by the arrival of food and drink, and the visits from the officials, the police and the border guards and Tan and Ky, then the boat crew and the captain's wife, not to mention the crowd of silent onlookers.

We could not believe the daily list of questions – the same questions, the same answers – repeated over and over again. We never seemed to make any progress. Tan and Ky explained that the reason we had provoked so much attention was because hardly anybody living on the island had ever seen a white person before. They also told us that we had been spotted on the reef by one of the captain's sons and that this was what had saved us.

Tan and Ky were very friendly and wanted to know all about Australia and New Zealand. They asked if they could bring some of their class groups to visit us and if we would talk to the children in English, because every child on the island, and in all of Vietnam, studied English. We said we would be more than happy to do this. Theirs was the only friendly communication we had each day and we relished it. Ky told us that the same monsoon that had blown us across the South China Sea for the past few weeks had claimed many lives on the mainland. He told us that the storm had prevented fishermen from going to sea and had stopped all supplies arriving from the mainland, so there were considerable food shortages on the island. All that the island could grow was garlic and chives. Even the staple, rice, had to come from the mainland. I still had no idea of our exact position and asked them how far we were from the mainland, but they didn't know, or rather could not tell us for security reasons.

From time to time the nurses stayed behind when the rest of the entourage had left, with other nurses joining them. It sometimes seemed as though every nurse in the hospital was in our room. They all laughed and giggled, holding their hands over their faces. One morning one of the girls shuffled forward and pointed at Steve and then back to herself and then her wedding ring finger. "Marry, marry?" she asked him.

Steve nodded his head with a big smile on his face and said, "Sure baby, I'll marry you." This provoked another burst of laughter. The blushing bride-to-be covered her face with her hands, laughing uncontrollably. This all got too much for our guards and they shooed the nurses out the door.

The captain's wife continued to bring us food and drinks each day, which included rice broth, soy drinks and oranges, all tasting fantastic. At first, other than eating, all I wanted to do was sleep. My body was skin and bone, the skin hanging loosely, and I was covered in all sorts of pimples, boils, sores, ulcers and welts. There was nothing much left of me: no muscles, nothing. Fuck me, I thought to myself. How did I make it through that surf and reef with this frail body? I wondered how much damage I had done to my organs. The stresses must have been huge; gigantic.

After two days on the island I had begun to feel incredibly weak, and concerned that still no one knew we were there. I was feeling depressed and dejected, and said to Steve, "Nobody knows where we are, still. I hope we don't keel over and die on the island without anybody knowing."

"Yeah, I have to say it's starting to get to me. I'm starting to feel pretty crook."

I tried guard number one again. "Telephone, telephone?" I asked, hand near my ear.

He barked back, "No telephone, no telephone! No, no, no!" He was beginning to sound like a broken record. He walked up to me and coming close to my face, shouted at me, "Where you from, what your name?" I told him to fuck off and smiled at him.

By the third night my bed was becoming increasingly uncomfortable. It had a steel frame and its base was a tightly stretched mattress of woven cane, as hard as nails. The only thing protecting my body from the cane was a single blanket. With no flesh on my body, I had nothing to protect my bones from the hard surface. I got the guard's attention and pointed at the bed, trying to make him understand what I wanted.

"Mattress, mattress," I kept on repeating, accompanied by all manner of gestures. He must have got the message because he left the room and went down the corridor.

He came back a few minutes later and crossed his arms and bellowed, "No mattress, no mattress! No, no, no!"

This guy was really starting to get up my nose. I folded the under blanket in half and that, at least, gave me two layers instead of one. It was still wide enough to fold it again so that there was a narrow strip of blanket running down the centre of the bed. Now I had four layers. I gingerly stretched out on my thin mini-mattress and covered myself with the other blanket. It was a little better, but not much. If there were no mattresses, surely I could find a few more blankets. That would be my first job tomorrow, I promised myself. The wind was still howling through and around the building, lashing the surrounding palms. The storm was not dying down. It was cold at night and I had the single blanket pulled up tight but I wasn't complaining. I thought of the living hell of the life raft and shook my head, unable to comprehend how I had made it through. There would be no more complaints about how tough life is from this man, I thought to myself.

The next morning I was sick to death of lying down and slowly eased myself up, swinging my legs to the floor. I grabbed the bedhead for support and pins and needles raged through my legs. Shit, that's not nice, I wailed to myself. I shook and wobbled my legs, trying to make the sensation go away, and it slowly eased. I was sitting up and could see out the window, and took in the scene. Below me was the hospital forecourt, a stone fence running around its perimeter, and then the road. There were a few small neat houses, some palm trees, a small field of green and then the ocean. Everywhere I looked it was green and lush, with bright flowers hanging on the vines. We were on the lee side of the island, the wind passing overhead and out to sea. The water was protected close to the island but peering further out I could see the white mist of the gale-swept ocean.

The fence, the road and the houses all looked solid. I brushed my hand across the wall next to my bed and it was solid too. What a wild case of sea legs I had had. My brain had convinced me we were on a floating island, but now everything was coming back to normal and the room had stopped rocking. I watched the island come awake. Bicycles and motorbikes started passing in front of the hospital, the flow quickly increasing. Before long there were hundreds of bicycles as well as motorbikes, with sometimes up to three people per motorbike, but most of them carrying two. Hundreds of school children in blue uniforms gaily laughed and chatted as they pushed their way along the road and nearly all of them glanced up at my open window. I waved to them and this led to more excited chatter, laughter and hands over mouths. I was interrupted from this pleasant scene by the morning rounds.

Later that day during the regular round of visits, an altercation broke out between one of the captain's sons and one of the guards. It became very heated, with the young man raising his fists in defiance. I was concerned as this was communist Vietnam and I knew that the system did not permit this type of rebellion against authority. The raised fist was too much for the guard. He grabbed the young man firmly by the arm and dragged him out of the room and marched him down the corridor, the family following quickly behind.

"Good on him for standing up to the prick," Steve said, and I had to agree. Just then I heard a phone ringing down the corridor and one of the doctors came into the room.

"Telephone, telephone," he said, and gestured for one of us to go with him.

Steve said, "You go." My heart was racing and I tried to get up, but I collapsed like a bag of potatoes on the floor. No way were my legs working. The doctor and a nurse helped me up and half carried me down the corridor.

Please let them still be on the line. "Hello," I said.

A female voice with an American accent replied, "Who am I speaking to?" I told her my name and that I was with my mate, Steve Freeman, and that we had been rescued by Vietnamese fishermen and were on an outlying island somewhere, but I didn't know where. She said, "My goodness, so it's true." She told me that she was following up on rumours spreading around the fishing towns of central Vietnam of two white men washed ashore and rescued somewhere off the coast. She introduced herself as Susan and told me she worked as a journalist for AAPT, based in Ho Chi Minh City. She asked about our health and what had happened, and I gave her a very brief run down of events. She listened in silence until I finished speaking. "Oh, well done boys, well done. This is big; has anybody contacted you, does anybody know you are there?" she asked.

"No, nobody, you're the first person I've spoken to."

"Leave it to me, give me all the numbers you can think of, family, friends, everybody." I had only one number to pass on, my parents' number in Naracoorte. The whole family including my children were gathering there for Christmas.

Susan repeated, "Well done boys, don't worry, help is on the way." I thanked her gratefully and she said she would keep in touch and hung up. Relief washed over me as I was helped back down the corridor. Finally, somebody in the outside world knew where we were. Now we just had to be patient and wait.

Susan did her job. The phone rang again and this time it was for Steve. He was helped down the corridor and came back about ten minutes later, all smiles. It had been the New Zealand Consul in Ho Chi Minh City. "He's calling my family right now," he said.

We were excitedly discussing the phone calls when the phone rang again. It was for Steve, and he was so happy when he came back that he was almost crying. "That was my sister, she's letting everyone know. They were all starting to get very worried and were thinking the worst," he said.

The phone rang again. "Mark Smith, Mark Smith," the doctor called. I was helped down the corridor for the second time and spoke to the assistant to the Consular General of Australia. What a welcome and familiar accent. He introduced himself as Nicholas Sergi, and he was concerned for our health and whether we were being treated and cared for properly. He told me that my family was being contacted as he spoke. This was the best news. I was so relieved that finally my children and family would know that I was safe. He apologised for not calling sooner but told me the media had gotten hold of the story and were blocking the lines with automatic and continuous redial. He advised me to sit tight and said he would call me the next day at the same time with news of evacuation plans.

At last things were moving and getting better. I hobbled back to my room supported by two nurses. All of this unfamiliar exercise had caused some movement inside me as well. My stomach cramped for the first time in fifteen days: I needed to go to the toilet. I was led past my room and around the corner to the bathroom. It was wet, cold and dark, and the wind was gusting through a shattered pane. I sat there shivering and tried, but nothing happened. I felt my backside and there was nothing, no muscles. How was I supposed to shit when I had no muscles? I sat there for ages trying, willing something to happen. One of the guards kept checking on me. "Piss off and leave me alone," I snapped at him, angered and embarrassed by his intrusion. Eventually and painfully, two small items splashed into the water; they felt and sounded like two concrete blocks. Thank fuck for that, I muttered to myself, exhausted by the effort. The guard helped me back to my bed.

"I've just had a shit," I happily declared to Steve, as if I was a toddler proudly showing off the contents of his potty for the first time. "At least that part is still working – just," I added.

I was getting settled back into bed when Tan, Ky and dozens of children filed into the room. We spent the next few hours happily chatting with the children; well, not really chatting, but they understood a lot of what we said and replied falteringly to some of our questions. We read to them from their English schoolbooks and they showed us their work. They sat in silence, enraptured as I slowly read to them, pointing at the words as I went. Tan and Ky were thrilled. They told me how great it was for these children to have the experience of talking and listening to us both. There was a knock on the door and the afternoon's rounds brought the visit to an end.

The doctors seemed satisfied with our progress. After the inspections, jabs, pills and leg dressing, one by one we were helped downstairs where we were put on a set of scales in the hospital foyer. I registered forty-four kilos, which shocked me. My weight had been steady at a bit over seventy kilos for years. I had lost nearly thirty kilos; no wonder I had been feeling a bit rooted. I was helped back up the stairs where dinner was waiting. Steve and I lay on our beds and excitedly talked abut the events of the day. We were soon to be rescued from the island.

It was getting dark and the wind was still roaring overhead. We had discovered the best way to communicate with the locals was by writing and drawing pictures, so I had scrounged a small pad and pen from Tan earlier in the day when the children were visiting. I drew a crude picture of a helicopter and showed it to guard number one, while making helicopter sounds and movements. Looking at the drawing and nodding his understanding, he stood up and crossed his arms over his chest. "No, no, no!"

I drew a plane on an airstrip and showed it to him. "No, no, no!"

I offered him a cigarette smuggled in by the captain's wife. "No, no, no!" he repeated.

I got bolder and offered him one of my precious oranges. "No, no, no." I offered a chocolate-covered wafer. "No, no, no." I was wasting my time. "Don't worry about it mate," I said to him. His training doctrine had clearly been rigid, permitting him to say nothing and receive nothing that might compromise him. I lay back down on my rock hard bed. On the raft our bodies had been suspended on a giant waterbed and the hardness of the hospital bed was still painful on my bones.

It had been a big day. We had had constant attention, constant visitors and phone calls. My family and children must know I was safe by now. The power went off as usual, the room falling into darkness. I savoured another orange in the blackness, and then pulled my blanket up close.

I was woken by the sound of Steve groaning. "You okay mate?" I called out.

"I feel like shit, terrible pains in my guts," he grunted.

I could see him in the shadows all hunched up, moaning in obvious pain. Steve's not the one to ever complain, he had hardly bitched at all on the raft. If he said he felt bad then he must seriously be bad. "You okay?" I called again.

More groans, then he cried out, "Fuck, I think I'm going to die!"

"What? You're not going to die man!" I struggled up, using the windowsill as support, and made my way across to his bed. He was doubled over in pain and kept saying, "I am going to die, I am going to die."

"No way mate, you can't die now!" But I was getting worried. I called out to the guard sleeping across the corridor. "Help, help, get a doctor!" The guards came running in with their torches flashing. "Doctor! Doctor!" I cried, pointing at Steve who was moaning in pain and clutching his chest and stomach. Guard number one replied, "No, no. No doctor."

The hospital was in total blackness and there was no doctor on duty; in fact, there was no one at all on duty. I repeated frantically, "Doctor, doctor!" pointing at Steve and running my fingers across my throat. There was a hurried discussion and guard number two disappeared down the corridor.

"Don't worry mate, hang in there, the doctor is coming," I said to Steve. I staggered across the room and out into the corridor, grabbing at whatever was available to hold myself up. I lurched into the guard's room and grabbed one of their thick, heavy sleeping bags and struggled back to Steve. "Here, lie on this mate, you'll be more comfortable." I tucked it under him and sat next to him waiting for a doctor to turn up.

He kept moaning, "I am going to die." I repeatedly told him "You are not going to die man, you are not going to die."

At long last two doctors bustled into the room, one of them carrying a kerosene lantern. A nurse followed them, not in uniform; she looked like she had just woken up. They started examining Steve, and one of the doctors issued some instructions to the nurse and she dashed off, returning quickly with needles and drugs. They gave Steve a jab and he managed to swallow the tablets. He collapsed on his bunk, breathing more steadily. The crisis seemed to be over. The doctors and the nurse left after making sure Steve had stabilised and was resting.

Guard number one pulled his sleeping bag out from under Steve and said, "no, no, no," as he marched out of the room with it. "Prick," I thought.

"You okay mate?" I called out to Steve.

"Yeah I'm okay. I hate the nights."

"I hate the nights," I echoed.

I was woken from a deep sleep in the morning by the sound of rain. Rain; get up, my brain cried. I opened my eyes and breathed a sigh of relief. We were safe in our hospital room and morning had arrived. After his bad night, Steve was the focus of attention during the morning rounds. He had come good but still complained about an aching stomach, and it must have been bad because he couldn't eat. As I dipped my spoon into the bowl I noticed the broth was thicker and had other finely chopped ingredients in it, and it tasted even better than before. The doctors watched me eat, and let me have another bowl. Eating was still the only thing I wanted to do and every mouthful was heaven.

I rested back on my bed and waited for the day's routine to start. The captain's wife produced a set of new clothes for us both, and the crowd all made a fuss as we changed into our new shorts and shirts, laughing and hiding their eyes. The phone had rung unanswered all through the night and also throughout the day. "Reporters, reporters," was all that the guards would tell us.

One of the doctors appeared at the door. "Mark Smith, Mark Smith," he repeated. I staggered out of bed and was helped down the corridor.

"Hello," I said into the mouthpiece.

"How are you faring, young man?" boomed a voice down the line. It was the unmistakable voice of Captain Brett Devine, a larger-than-life figure on Sydney's waterfront who owned a large marine construction and salvage business. I had worked for Brett on many occasions, captaining his pride and joy, the thirty-five metre ocean-going salvage tug, the *MV Wheeler*. Brett was a tough but fair operator, for whom nothing was too hard or too challenging. Above all, Brett was a family man, and if you worked for Brett you were part of his family.

"Brett, how are you mate? How did you get through? I thought the phones were blocked by reporters."

"Don't worry about it mate, I called a friend." Brett had friends everywhere. He asked how I was and what happened. I gave him a quick run down, finishing up with us being weathered in on the island, not knowing how long we would be there. "Don't worry, young man, stay put. I'm organising a team right now to fly to Vietnam, and I'll charter a plane or a helicopter and come and get you."

I talked a bit more about our experience while Brett listened silently. "Shit man, you've been through hell. Don't worry, I'm coming to get you." After checking if he could make any calls for me to family and friends, we hung up. I was smiling to myself as I hobbled back to our room. You could always rely on Captain Brett Devine when you were in a fix.

Just after I got back, Tan turned up. He gave me more writing paper and asked me to write a letter to the senior party members of the island; setting out the treatment we had received during our time here. He told me that I had to deliver this letter at a meeting to be held the following day.

The guards came in and Tan interpreted for us. A naval vessel that was coming to get us had been turned back due to the bad weather. This was disappointing news but I tried to remain calm. We were alive and being well cared for, and that, after all, was what mattered. Tan said he would return the next day and assist me at the meeting.

In the meantime, two nurses had been struggling down the corridor with a large tub and a few minutes later they turned up with a cake of soap and a small hand towel. "Wash, wash," they said, laughing and smiling. They pointed to me first and helped me to the bathroom. This would be my first bath in sixteen days. My skin was itchy and still covered in salt and it would be sheer luxury to be clean again. I sat on a low stool in the small, dark room, sponging warm water and soap lather all over my neck, feeling it run down my body. I used every drop of water to slowly rinse the suds away. It felt really good. I struggled back into my clothes and hobbled back to our room. I was wobbling and staggering like a drunk but starting to get around shakily by myself.

The bath did wonders for my morale. I was tired and looking forward to sleeping in my dry bed with my body clean and wearing new clothes. I pulled the blanket up over my head.

"Telephone, telephone," brought me back to my senses. I hobbled down the corridor. It was Nicholas. We quickly discussed the day's events and then he gave me the bad news. The weather was deteriorating even further and it didn't look as though they would be able to get us off the island for another few days yet. I groaned. He told me about the aborted attempt by the navy and I told him I had already heard about it. He enquired about the weather conditions on the island and I told him the wind was a good thirty knots and gusting. But he did have some good news. He had spoken to my mother and she was over the moon to learn that I was okay. She had sent me all her love and said to tell me that everybody was waiting for my return. He thanked me for my patience and assured me that everything that could be done was being done.

I explained to him that the staff and guards were ignoring the phones and that I was concerned that important calls and information might not get through. Nicholas said that he had made special arrangements to get this call through and that he would do the same again tomorrow. "Just sit tight and look after yourself," he said as we hung up.

I got back to my room just in time for the afternoon rounds and as these were progressing I filled Steve in on the news. While I had been sleeping, Steve had also taken a couple of calls, one of them from the New Zealand consul and another one from his sister, and we happily shared all our gossip. I told him about the call from Brett Devine and he told me that even with the best of intentions, Brett would never get permission from the Vietnamese government to allow such a mission, one of the reasons being that these islands were militarily sensitive. So that would put an end to that.

The next morning the wind had not eased and was whipping at the palm trees across the road. There would be no rescue today, I could be sure of that, I sighed. I seriously wanted to get home. I wanted all of this to come to an end. Steve stirred and opened his eyes. "Morning, mate," I said.

"Morning. What's it like out there?"

"Up to shit, still blowing, with a big sea running. They won't be getting us out today."

"Yeah mate, I can hear the wind."

We were both seamen, so we didn't need to be told that being picked up today was out of the question. No good complaining or bitching, the weather was the weather; we couldn't do anything to change it.

I was content to sit and look out the window until the doctors and nurses arrived for their morning rounds. My legs were showing good signs of recovery; the swollen and angry red lines were fading and the wound itself was starting to dry and heal. After the doctors and their entourage had left, I sat by the window and using the sill as a rest, I started on my speech. It was easy to write; the bravery, care and compassion shown to us by the people of Ly Son Island had been overwhelming.

I was finishing up when Tan and another gentleman entered the room. Tan introduced his colleague as the official party photographer, and explained that he was here to take some videos and still shots. The guards arrived with another set of new clothes, this time long trousers and cotton shirts with collars and buttons. We dressed for the occasion and then the doctors and nurses came back in and the photographer began filming. He took shots of the doctor listening to my chest, shots of a nurse taking my blood pressure, shots of a nurse administering an injection, shots of us eating food, drinking coffee – it went on and on. It was all quite hilarious; everybody was laughing, even the head doctor. Then it was a wrap and the photographer packed up his gear and said his goodbyes.

After they had all left, I made shaving motions to one of the nurses. Seventeen days without a shave was way too long for me and my face was itching. She nodded her head and went to find a razor, a packet of blades and a bar of soap. Off I wobbled to the bathroom and looked at myself in a small mirror. This was not going to be easy, with seventeen days growth on a hollow and sore-covered face. I started the chore and the razor got totally blocked on the first pass. By the time the guards came to check up on me a few minutes later, I had only cleared a tiny patch next to my ear. They offered to help, which was quite something. We discarded the razor and attempted it with just the blades. It was a painful process but after a lot of scratching away I declared the ordeal over. I checked the results in the mirror. It was not a close shave by any standards, but I did look much better. I patted my sagging face and thanked the guards.

When I got back to my room Steve was sitting up, happily hopping into an orange. He was all smiles as he had just taken another call from his sister and from the New Zealand consul. The latest news was that there was something about money being needed to pay our hospital bill, all of our costs on the island and the cost of the boat coming to fetch us. Money? I didn't like the sound of that. I certainly didn't have any. I decided not to worry about it; someone would surely help us get off the island.

After being cooped up in this room for nearly five days and before that, eleven days on our knees in a raft, we both needed to go for a walk and I had wanted to check things out. I wrapped myself in a blanket and wandered out into the corridor, taking an orange with me, just in case. The guards were resting on their beds and number two looked up as we passed. "Telephone, telephone," I said to him, as I gestured with my hand to my ear. He nodded and we shuffled past down the corridor. We made a beeline for the stairs, clutching the banisters for support, as we made our way to the foyer. A couple of nurses gave us surprised and curious looks from a small dispensary. We decided to split up; one of us might get away!

"I'm going out the front and down the road," said Steve.

"No worries mate, I'll just go out the back and have a wander about."

"Okay, see you later mate."

We split up and I shuffled along a covered concrete path between the buildings. The hospital looked pretty bare and empty and decay was showing everywhere. I was enjoying myself, wandering about on solid land for the first time since leaving Hong Kong. Everything seemed so long ago – Hong Kong, the sinking, the raft. I had barely given these a thought since arriving on the island. I walked past the buildings and came to the perimeter wall, where large sections had long ago fallen down and lay in big long slabs amongst the leaves. I stepped carefully over one of the slabs and walked, or rather hobbled, into a field of chives. They were growing in neat rows and I walked between them as I made my way up a gentle slope. I very quickly ran out of steam, and stopped to look at the twin peaks of the old volcano.

I turned around to survey the view. The hospital was below me and there was a large school next to it. No wonder I had seen so many school children every day. A road wound its way around the edge of the island, with clusters of small houses scattered along its sides. Everywhere I looked it was green and lush.

I made my way back down the hill to the fence and had just started down the concrete path when two worried young nurses came running up. They supported me on each side and hustled me along. I didn't understand a word of their worried-sounding chatter, but it was clear I was being scolded. As fast as they could they got me up the stairs and into my room. A very flustered guard number one burst in. "No, no, no!" he shouted. He pointed at Steve's bed. "Where Steve, where Steve?" he shouted again. I told him I had just been to the toilet and I didn't have a clue where Steve was. Had he tried the telephone, I asked. He didn't understand a word. He just kept shouting, "no, no, no!" and then rushed out the door.

About ten minutes later a rather sheepish looking Steve was ushered back into the room by guard number one, who plonked him down on his bed and shouted, "no, no, no!"

"Alright, alright! Don't get your knickers in a knot. There's no harm done, we just went for a little walk," I said to him.

It didn't register. "No, no, no!" was his only response. He angrily left the room. Steve and I laughed about our little escapade. Guard number one had picked up Steve about half a mile down the road.

Tan arrived in the early afternoon for the meeting with the senior party officials. He led me into a big room at the head of the stairs that I had noticed earlier. It was empty, with a large table in the centre of the room and posters, photographs and maps covering the walls. Glancing around, I found a large chart of the island hanging on the wall. I busily studied this and located the reef that we had come ashore on and the road to the hospital. There was an airstrip on the far southern end of the island. So, I thought, they can land planes here.

My thoughts were interrupted by the arrival of all the dignitaries, uniforms, brass and suits; even the official photographer. Everybody was ushered into position and the proceedings commenced, with the video rolling. Tan asked me to stand up and read my letter. I stood up and began slowly reading, stopping frequently so that Tan could interpret. It wasn't a very long speech. I described and applauded the bravery of the fishermen who saved us and I spoke of the care we had received on the beach. I told of the compassion, skills and care of the hospital staff, and how grateful we were for the services that the hospital had provided. I spoke of the professional way in which the different authorities had treated us and finished by thanking the entire population of Ly Son Island and all who had been involved in saving our lives. Everybody was smiling.

The head party member then stood up and also delivered a short speech, which Tan also interpreted. He thanked me for my words and welcomed me to Ly Son Island. He was happy to see that we were recovering and assured us that everything was being done to try to get us home. Everybody clapped and the meeting was over. The party chief came across to me and shook my hand. Then from a side table, he presented me with two large boxes wrapped in colourful foil. I thanked him again and the meeting broke up.

I shuffled back to my room with our presents. "One each," I said to Steve, tossing him one of the boxes. We tore off the foil wrappings and opened them up. They consisted of clothes and food – cakes, biscuits and lollies. We opened the small boxes and started feasting away, until I was interrupted by a call from Nicholas. I told him that it was still blowing and he said that the forecast for the following day was still bad but that the wind had dropped below twenty-five knots. He had also spoken to Kurt who was sending an assistant with an open chequebook to pay for our trip home. This was good news. He warned me about a media scrum that was gathering in Quang Ngai, our destination on the Vietnamese mainland.

Steve was happy with the news about Kurt's assistant coming to help us home. My appetite was growing every second and I spent the afternoon eating rice, rolls, cakes, biscuits and sweets, and drinking coffee. The evening rounds came and went with more food and attention. As I was preparing to go to sleep that night, it occurred to me that I hadn't seen the captain's wife all day.

It blew and rained all night. In the middle of the night, I awoke with stomach cramps, due to my having overeaten. I wrapped myself in a blanket and guided by the feeble light of a kerosene lamp, I paddled through the pools of cold water in my bare feet to the bathroom. A rush of wind gusting through a broken pane blew the lantern out, and so I sat for hours in the cold darkness, doubled up with spasms of pain. Everything bad happens at night I thought, when I finally got myself back to bed. I hate the nights.

The next day arrived and passed with the usual array of check ups and visitors, and Steve forever flirting and receiving more and more offers of marriage from the nurses.

My cramps had disappeared and there was no stopping me when the food came in, happily finishing every last morsel and enjoying it too. As the last of the visitors were leaving, the captain's wife appeared in the room. She was drenched from the rain but did not seem to be the slightest bit bothered by this. She took our washed clothes from a plastic bag and gave them to us. As she handed me my shorts she quickly looked around to see if anyone was watching and pointed to notes and names written in ink on the inside of them. She then thrust a piece of paper in my hand, with more names and numbers, and indicated I should hide this from the guards. I folded the shorts carefully and tucked the note in with other papers I had collected during my time at the hospital, nodding my understanding.

My communication with the captain's wife was improving, not through language but by signing and hastily drawn diagrams. I learned that the police had taken her son away due to his confrontation with the guard, and that she had been reprimanded for bringing us food and drinks.

Nicholas phoned again that afternoon with some good news. The wind was expected to drop overnight and the navy was planning to get us off the island the following day. This was music to my ears. He said that Kurt's assistant, David, had spoken to him on the phone from Ho Chi Minh City and that he and the New Zealand consulate official were planning on flying to Danang in the morning to await developments. I still had absolutely no idea where we were, but it looked as though we might be finally getting off the island. He spoke briefly on issues facing us once we were back on the mainland. The hospital and rescue bills, visas, temporary passports, travel documents, formal handovers and other things – it was all too confusing. I let it go over my head. I would deal with things as they came up.

It was all good. Tomorrow; tomorrow I might take another step towards getting home, I thought. As I sat at my window watching the locals going home, I noticed that the wind had died noticeably, with only an occasional gust rattling through the building. Please lie down wind, please lie down I urged, as I looked out to sea in the fading light.

That night seemed to be the longest night and at first light I was up and at the open window. The wind had dropped – it must have been under twenty-five knots, twenty even – and there was only a small swell breaking at the edge of the reef. The boat must come today. It had to come.

We got through the morning's routine without any fuss, and I was hungrily tucking into a big bowl of rice when guard number one came into the room and announced, "boat coming, boat coming!" What a relief! We were going to get off the island! I tried to ask what time but got no response. Guard number one either didn't know or didn't understand my question. He indicated that we should put on our best clothes, the long trousers and shirts, and pointed down the corridor. There was going to be another meeting.

Guard number two brought in two boxes and a small plastic bag that contained two pairs of sneakers and socks. As we were getting dressed the guards sanitised the room. They gathered up all of our notes and paperwork and searched the room, looking through our clothes. Guard number one found the shorts with the names and telephone numbers of our friends inside. He showed them to me and said, "no, no, no." I prayed that I hadn't got the captain's wife and her family into more trouble.

The shoes felt strange on my feet. I clumped over to the window and sat there watching and waiting. "Telephone, telephone!" came an excited voice from the door. It was Nicholas, who told me that the boat was on its way and that he was arranging to meet us when it docked. He said that he would be accompanied by Steve's mate from the New Zealand consulate, and Dave. He told me that there was a lot of media interest and that local and global reporters had gathered in Danang. Two reporters, one from AAPT and another from Reuters, had managed to get on the boat. It didn't really matter to us. The boat was coming at last.

We hung up. I got back to the room to find it chock-a-block with people – the captain, his wife, the crew and their wives and friends. Steve had told them what the guards had done and was busily scribbling down names and numbers, hiding the bits of paper in his trousers. 'Good on you,' I thought. It would be a tragedy if we were to lose contact with these wonderful people. Luckily, Steve had finished when guard number one came into the room. "Boat arrives, boat arrives," the guard said.

We all sat there and waited. One hour passed, two hours passed. The tension was rising. I kept looking out the window. What was the hold up? Why the delay? Another hour crept past. I was like a cat on a hot tin roof, trembling with nerves and excitement as I paced around the room and up and down the corridor. Finally, I heard a multitude of tooting horns and looking out the window, saw dozens and dozens of motorcycles entering the hospital courtyard. People were coming from all directions. I spotted the reporters setting up their cameras. The show had begun.

Tan pushed into the room and asked if I still had my speech and I told him the guards had taken it. He said he would find it and rushed off. The next minute the two reporters, large video cameras on their shoulders, jostled their way into the room, filming as they came. They introduced themselves – they were an American and a Frenchman – and started asking questions. Then we were all being pushed out of the room. The corridor was crowded as we made our way to the central hall and Tan pushed his way to our side and guided us into the room.

All the dignitaries were there: the doctors, the party chief, the border guard, officers, the police and other VIPs. Along with these were the official party from the navy boat – army and naval uniforms and lots of brass and ribbons. Crowded into the room were also the official photographer and the two journalists. Our rescuer, the captain, was sitting between Steve and myself, with Tan on my other side. The room came to order.

Tan explained that we were now to be officially handed over to the army. The island's job was finished. I didn't understand much of what went on but there was lots of paperwork being scrutinised and stamped, and passed from person to person. Everyone seemed happy enough and the paperwork was completed. At a nod from the party chief, Tan asked me to read out my letter once again. I stood up and retold the story about my time on Ly Son Island, sincerely thanking everybody for the expert, professional and compassionate care we had received. I thanked the captain next to me for his bravery and friendship. Everybody was smiling and beaming at Tan's translation. Everything had worked out well, everybody had done their jobs successfully, and everyone had received kudos. Lots of official photographs were taken. I noticed the captain's wife pressed against the glass of the door, with tears in her eyes as Steve and I were photographed next to her husband. A few short speeches from the dignitaries and it was all over.

We were jostled outside and made our way downstairs, carrying our belongings in plastic bags. The crowd was huge, everybody pressing in on us, touching us, waving goodbye. It was as if we belonged to the island and nobody wanted us to leave. The head doctor came up and we embraced. I thanked him from the bottom of my heart for all that he and his staff had done, and he had a tear in his eye as well. Suddenly it was sad to be leaving, to be saying goodbye. The captain's wife rushed up and gave me a big hug. It was all happening too fast. I was plonked on to the back of a motorbike. It sounded its horn and we lurched forward.

I looked back at the sea of waving hands. We were on our way; next stop Vietnamese mainland. I enjoyed the bike ride, taking in the island and all the people stopping what they were doing and waving as we went past. The journos were sitting backwards behind their riders, zooming their cameras in my face.

The small wharf was crowded; supply boats had finally made it to the island. There were sacks of rice, boxes of food and vegetables lying everywhere. Pigs squealed in small cane baskets as we threaded our way through and were helped onto the boat.

When everybody was aboard, the engines fired in a cloud of black smoke and we were away. I saw the captain and his wife standing in the crowd on the jetty. Everybody waved until there was nothing to wave at. I stood at the stern of the small patrol boat and watched the island growing smaller. I thought of the twenty or thirty thousand people who lived there. Tan had told me that most of them had never left the island.

I asked one of the journos how long it had taken them to get across here and it was only a couple of hours. It had been an intense and busy day, and I suddenly felt very tired, hungry and thirsty. I found a bunk in the fo'c'sle where the ride of the boat sent me straight to sleep. An hour or so later, the change of the boat's motion brought me to my feet and I climbed out onto the deck. The sight of the Vietnamese mainland, flat and green along the coastal plains, greeted me. A rugged chain of mountains appeared misty blue on the far horizon. Dozens of small fishing boats were all around us as we entered an estuary, with hundreds more tied up dozens deep from the shore. I shook my head; how could there be that many fish left in the sea, I sadly wondered. We tied up alongside a similar craft at a small wooden jetty and everybody clambered ashore and the journos took more photos. It was hot and humid and I needed to find some shade and something to drink. I found a small shop, which was just an open shack with two low tables and a couple of stools. A small counter held its wares. The journos shouted us a drink, wanting us to tell them our story.

It wasn't long before a white minibus stopped outside. Nicholas, the New Zealand consular official and David introduced themselves, along with Nicholas's assistant, a young Vietnamese woman. Dave looked the odd one out, not quite what I had expected. He was quite young, maybe mid-twenties, with curly, sun-bleached hair down to his shoulders, a Hawaiian shirt, board shorts and sandals; a surfie, I thought to myself. He was excited to see us and asked us if we were all right. It was so good to be speaking the same language again and there was so much to talk about, too much. But the army was waiting so we were bundled into the minibus and in convoy, drove away from the estuary. Dave said it was a short ride to Quang Ngai, maybe half an hour at the most. I watched the countryside roll past, taking in my first look at Vietnam. Night was falling as we entered the city. I couldn't believe it had been seven days since we had been dragged out of our damaged raft.

Vietnam and Home

Shortly after, our little convoy turned off a wide, tree-lined avenue and into a sprawling military base. We stopped at a group of buildings close to the entrance. Nicholas told us that until the formal handover had occurred, we were still guests of the Vietnamese   government and in the care of the Vietnamese army. The building we stopped at was an officers' hostel and several restaurants and eateries surrounded a courtyard. A group of army officers came up to us and started giving directions while Meanne (Nicholas's assistant) interpreted. We were to register at the hostel and then appear before a press conference. As we entered the hostel, Meanne told Steve and me that we had to stay in the confines of the building and courtyard during our stay. I just went with the flow.

The foyer of the hotel was filled with people, and there were official photographers, questions, press photographers and more questions. In the background, files and paperwork were being scrutinised and passed between officials. I was tired and hungry. Finally, two guards escorted us upstairs and showed us to our room. Unreal. There were two large double beds with mattresses, sheets, blankets and pillows, not to mention the large bathroom with a full size tub. Bath, dinner and bed; this was going to be too good. The only annoying thing was that two guards came in, sat down in our lounge chairs and started watching the television, helping themselves to our stash of cakes and lollies. That was a bit much; Steve and I didn't mind sharing but the guards were definitely invading our privacy. But no amount of persuasion or argument would budge them. They seemed happy where they were and besides, they couldn't understand one word we were saying.

Dave appeared with a bag full of toiletries. Bugger the guards; I was going to have a tub. It would be sheer luxury. I was lying on my bed waiting while Steve had his turn in the bathroom, when there was a knock at the door. It was Dave again, who handed me a phone and told me it was Kurt. Kurt was happy that we were safe and sound but immediately started asking me about the sinking. Throughout my ordeal on the raft and during my partial recovery on the island, my brain had been in no state to give this subject much thought. But while there were still many unanswered questions, I knew what I had seen – the massive inrushing of water. Kurt came up with all sorts of theories as to what he thought must have happened and I listened politely to them all, but it was apparent to me that Kurt was really more interested in the insurance issues than our fate. It was academic. I had departed Hong Kong with all the correct paperwork and there had been a terrible accident resulting in the loss of his vessel. I told Kurt that we would sort it all out on my return to Sydney. The main thing was that we were alive and getting better. I hung up. It was dinnertime.

There was a bit of confusion when we all gathered in the foyer of the hostel. It turned out that Steve and I were strictly under the care of the Vietnamese army and as such, we would be dining as guests of the Vietnamese army to the exclusion of Nicholas, the New Zealand official, David and Meanne, who were all a bit miffed by this. Dave suggested that the army was just milking the system and that he would be billed for the event along with everything else. If it was milking the system then they certainly did it well. Steve and I were joined by ten smiling Vietnamese officers and the feasting and drinking began. Again, we couldn't understand a word of anything that was said, but our hosts seemed to thoroughly enjoy themselves. There were platters of food and crates of beer, with anything that looked remotely empty being replaced immediately. There was too much of everything and before long my mind and body shouted, stop! It had been a huge day. I nudged Steve who agreed. We thanked everybody for the meal and their hospitality and hobbled across the courtyard to the hostel. This was the most walking I had done since Hong Kong and it was beginning to tell.

I knocked on Nicholas's door to let him know we were safely back. I found him and Dave discussing one of the issues facing our repatriation: the bill. Dave was strongly protesting the amounts of many of the entries on a long list spread before them. I glanced at the list and saw that many entries were followed by numbers with lots of zeros. I didn't understand the Vietnamese currency, so I was a little bit worried about what the cost had come to. I knew it had cost the Australian government hundreds of thousands of dollars to rescue Tony Bullimore from the middle of the ocean a few years ago. Their discussion had reached a bit of an impasse. I piped up, "Look, I don't really want to know, but how much in Australian dollars has all this cost?"

Dave said, "You're right, you don't want to know, but it looks like about two and a half."

Two and a half, two and a half, I thought. $2,500,000? $250,000? $25,000? Which was it? I got bolder and asked, "Two and a half what?"

"$2,500 Australian dollars," Dave replied.

I was stunned. Dave was arguing the point over a few measly dollars. After all that these people had done for us, it seemed ridiculous. Steve reacted quickly. He stood up and said, "I've heard enough, I'm going to bed."

I followed him through the door but before leaving I looked at Nicholas, who seemed a bit embarrassed and was being diplomatically quiet. I said, "I'm sure you gentlemen will be able to sort this problem out."

As we climbed into our beds, Steve said, "I was going to belt him if I had stayed one second longer." I had seen the look in his eyes as we'd left the others. He would have. "Not wrong, mate," I replied. Open chequebook indeed, I thought to myself as I drifted to sleep in total luxury.

The next morning it was time for our official handover. Again, there was the mass of uniforms in the foyer and courtyard. Steve and I were moved from jeep to jeep until the right combination of drivers, vehicles and personnel was achieved. We set off in a convoy of three vehicles, the sentry at the gate smartly saluting as he raised the boom. We turned left into the traffic, drove down the road, made a right turn across the wide, separating park and right again, back the way we had come on the other side of the avenue. Passing the hostel we did the same u-turn at the next intersection and were smartly saluted again by the same guard as he raised the boom. We stopped outside a large hall about fifty metres from the hostel! We could have walked and saved all the fuss, I thought.

The formalities began, as always, filmed and taped by the official photographers. At the appropriate time I was asked to repeat the speech I had made on the island. It was good to be able to explain to the dignitaries the bravery, compassion and care we had received from their kinsmen, who had undoubtedly saved our lives. I noted the genuine happiness in the generals' and party chiefs' faces as this was slowly translated by the interpreters. Strange how life is, I thought to myself. Not so long ago Australia was at war with Vietnam and we were killing the very same people who had saved us from death and nurtured us back to health.

With handshakes and more boxes of goodies and smiles for the cameras, it was all over. As we drove out of Quang Nai in the consular minivan an hour later, Nicholas remarked on how smoothly and quickly everything had gone. These sorts of things can take days, he explained. He told us our plan.

We were driving to Danang, which had the closest regional airport, and would then be flying to Ho Chi Minh City in the evening. I tried to enjoy the ride and the conversation but I was having other problems. My knees were locking up and were becoming very painful.

We stopped for lunch at Hoi An, a town doubly renowned for its fashion and clothing industry as well as its mixture of French and Vietnamese cuisine. It was all very nice, a place to return to some day, but my knees man, they were giving me serious trouble. After lunch we had to walk back to the minibus as it was pedestrians only in central Hoi An. I was stumbling along at the back of the group when my knees finally gave up. I was rooted to the spot, spasms of pain shooting up and down my legs. I was going nowhere. Everybody else disappeared around the corner and I just stood there, unable to move. A few minutes later a worried-looking Meanne rushed back around the corner and I was loaded onto a three-wheeled bicycle/pram contraption, and with a mixture of relief and embarrassment I was deposited back at our van.

Nicholas decided we should head straight to the doctor at Danang. It was a small private hospital, modern and well equipped. Steve and I received a thorough going over and eventually, a nurse injected my knees with what the doctor described as something new, but which worked. He was right, and by the time we got to the airport in the fading light, all of the pain had gone.

There was a hold up at the airport. Even though Nicholas and Meanne were armed with their diplomatic passes and a sheath of paperwork covering our presence, Steve and I still had no valid internal travel documents. A tense time followed, along with phone calls and meetings behind closed doors. It was with great relief that we were eventually given clearance, minutes before our scheduled flight, and it was late on the Friday night when we were dropped off at a hotel in central Ho Chi Minh City. Christmas Day was on Sunday and Nicholas told me that he could issue me a temporary passport during the weekend, but could not arrange for my exit visa until Monday at the earliest. This was to be handled by the local authorities.

Christmas came and went. I didn't stray much from my room, leaving only to buy food and drinks. I was happy sitting quietly by myself, marvelling at being alive. My mind drifted back to the happy times in Hong Kong. Would I ever see Florida again?

Monday was spent with Meanne who took us from office to office, gathering our travel and exit documents. By the afternoon, Dave was finally able to arrange our travel home and booked us on a flight leaving the next evening, Ho Chin Minh City to Sydney direct. By now, I just wanted to get home and see my children. Nothing had really sunk in yet, and the enormity of my struggle and the events of the last thirty-two days had become blurred and confused in my mind.

We landed at Sydney's Kingsford Smith Airport on the 28th of December 2005. Thirty-four days of my life had passed in the most incredible manner and for me the journey wasn't over until I was home. I spent a frustrating afternoon and night in Sydney. Kurt, who was not at the airport to meet us, met us later in the day and he seemed only to be interested in the insurance angle of the disaster.

I asked Dave if there was somewhere we could go to sleep. In the last few days I had learnt a bit about Kurt from Dave. It wasn't all good. Dave managed one of Kurt's investments, a rambling backpackers' hostel close to Bondi Junction. It was midway between Christmas and the New Year and the place was chock-a-block full with nearly sixty young, partying backpackers. Dave said he would be partying all night so I could have his room, which happened to be on the top floor of the building, up endless rickety stairs. The effects of the injection that I received in Danang had worn off long ago and I collapsed into bed, wondering how much longer it would be before I got home. I went to sleep exhausted and hungry.

We had a five-thirty appointment for an interview with a television breakfast show the next morning. Returning from the studio about seven o'clock, I found the door to Dave's room locked. A very groggy Dave answered after a few taps. "I've just got to bed, can you give me a couple of hours?" he begged. I wasn't feeling the best myself. Just as he closed the door I asked if I could borrow a towel and grab a shower and he directed me to the bathroom a few flights down. Being a backpackers' hostel there was no soap, so I grabbed up small bits I could find lying around the communal bathroom and did the best I could.

Everything was quiet downstairs – it had been a big night of partying and being a backpackers', all the food was locked away. Even the kitchen was locked. I was famished; I had had nothing to eat since getting off the plane yesterday. Even the television crew had eaten homemade biscuits in front of us without offering us any. I had a few dollars in my pocket that Dave had given me for phone calls yesterday so I set off in search of food. I hobbled to a shopping centre I had noticed and entered the first place I could find open. I promptly burnt my mouth on my first mouthful of chips that were straight from the boiling oil. Shit, shit, shit! I just wanted to get home.

Back at Kurt's backpackers' I knocked Dave up again. "Please man, just get me a ticket home. Come on, you can sleep all day after that." He eventually got himself organised and we walked back to the shopping centre and after a bit of mucking around, I managed to get my flight home to Hobart, leaving about four o'clock in the afternoon. We made our way slowly back to Dave's place, reminiscing over the past seven or eight days. I thanked him for all his help and promised to keep in touch.

I used the last of my money to call Brett Devine. I told him where I was and that I had to catch a flight home in a few hours' time. I added that I was broke and hungry. He said he had read the papers and seen me on television. He told me to stay put and he was coming to get me. While I was waiting for Brett I bade good luck and farewell to Steve. We didn't have much to say, we had been through it all together. He was looking forward to going home to New Zealand the next day.

Brett arrived and took me to a restaurant. Sitting, eating

and talking in the restaurant for a few hours did wonders for me. At the airport Brett thrust $500 into my hand and a mobile phone. "Have a rest and call me when you're ready. I have a job in mind for you," he said, as we shook hands.

I couldn't believe it. I was on the last leg of my trip home. The living hell of the life raft flashed through my mind. I knew there were still many questions to be answered and issues to be faced. But a few hours later it didn't matter any more. As I entered the Hobart terminal I was hit by two human cannonballs: Sophie and Daniel. Daddy had come home.

Apart from all the issues I had to face in reliving this story, I became aware of how important a well-designed and equipped life raft is.

Life rafts can be improved and their owners must be better educated. I would feel for anybody found in my predicament – experiencing the disheartening realisation that their life raft, their last refuge, has failed them. Why should a sailor have hope ripped from him because his raft is practically useless against the raging sea?

In retrospect I think that life rafts have come a long way over the years, but I believe that they and their equipment can be significantly enhanced.

My personal experience has resulted in considerable innovative and practical improvements that can be incorporated into a new era of life raft design.

If these improvements can help save the life of even one person lost at sea, then everything I have experienced will have been worthwhile.

Mark Smith.